Please note that CMI Publishers style capitalizes certain pronouns in Scripture that refer to the Father, Son and the Holy Spirit. We choose to do this out of respect and reverence for the Godhead even though this may differ from some publisher's styles.

Take note that the name satan and related names are not capitalized. We choose not to acknowledge him even to the point of violating grammatical rules.

Celebration Ministries, Incorporated
P.O. Box 2605
Clarksville, Indiana 47131 U.S.A.

For Worldwide Distribution, Printed in the U.S.A.

Thousandfold Principle
ISBN: 13: 978-0-9770560-2-6
Copyright © 2011 by John W. Smith, Jr.

This book is available for distribution. For more information call, 812-949-9595

Or reach us on the Internet:
www.johnwsmithjr.com

This book may also be downloaded on our website or through various epub and pdf book readers that use the DRM protocol including but not limited to: iPad, Sony Reader, Kindle, Nook, KOBO.

ACKNOWLEDGEMENTS

The Lord placed an anointing on me to write this book for the generation at hand and the generations to come. The Anointing of God embedded this book in my spirit so that I could document the things He has revealed to me concerning the release of the provision for end time purposes.

In order to do this it took several months of diligence and research to complete the text within its pages. God has blessed me with wonderful folks that not only believe in this project, but have sown into it as well.

This significant group of gifted people has helped me to accomplish my purpose in ministry throughout the years. Most recently they have increased their efforts to bring this book to fruition. Without their contribution this study would never have touched a page.

To my wife Darlene who was custom made to listen to my ideas and encourage me to finish, I salute you and I love you. This book is dedicated to you and may God reward you for the tireless hours you have put into the vision of my heart. You are special beyond description. You are my friend and co-laborer in the Gospel.

To my son JJ, I applaud your strength and think about the gift that is you every day. You have weathered through life's toughest battles and have shown the faith of God in your life to be a true force to be reckoned with. You have listened to my messages thousands of times in the edit and production rooms. The impartation of the anointing in those words is your greatest inheritance from me.

To my daughters, Holly and Stephanie, you are the fairest in the land. Your steady stream of laughter has kept me strong and has cheerfully humbled me in my times of stress and pressure. You are God's reward to your mother and me. I love you both.

To all of the wonderful partners and friends that have communicated with me through giving and receiving, may God richly bless you and impart the anointing of the Holy Spirit upon this book and my life into your heart forever.

Most importantly, to God the Father who gave me the faculties, revelation and wisdom to complete this book for the Kingdom and His glory. May many millions of lives be changed through the power to get wealth that establishes your covenant promises to all of us who will believe them.

I love you.

DEDICATION

This book is dedicated to the men and women of faith that gave their lives for the purpose of educating and mentoring the Body of Christ with the Rhema word of God. Many of them stepped out and taught on prosperity when it wasn't acceptable among the religious leaders of their day.

I thank God for these pillars of faith that built foundational truth for the people to take hold of and live by. I have personally benefited from their countless hours of study of the word of God.

I also dedicate this book to the visionaries of Christian TV. If they had not stepped out and built the stations, networks and distribution centers of quality Christian TV program, the world would be a much darker place.

CONTENTS

FOREWORD

I am thankful and grateful for my husband, John. The Lord blessed my life greatly with a man of God that stands on the word of God and nothing else. John is a faithful husband and a tremendous father to our children and grandchildren. His love and understanding heart has brought much joy and love into our home.

I believe this book is a mandate by the Holy Spirit for such a time as this. The revelation knowledge of the thousandfold principle is for every person. Believers need to be operating in this flow of wisdom and wealth to get the assignment of preaching the gospel done. The number one response we hear in our international prayer center, letters from telecast viewers, and our church congregation is, "We can understand John's teachings." People love the method by which he teaches and the style by which he presents. God gave John a great gift of "teaching" the word.

Many of the people who contact this ministry remark over and over again that they have never heard anything like it before. Many lives have been transformed because of John's willing to obey the voice of the Lord. I believe as you read this book you too will say I understand more than ever about sowing into the Kingdom of God at thousandfold measure.

I pray in the name of Jesus that as you read this book you will receive the revelation knowledge of the thousandfold principle. I pray that the impartation of this word will forever change your life. The Word of God is the whole truth that will set you free.

Mrs. Darlene Smith

INTRODUCTION

The word thousand is recorded in the King James Bible 521 times. The word thousandfold is only mentioned one time. The word thousandfold is hidden in the scripture in the book of Psalms as the word thousands in Psalm 144:13 where King David prays for God to bring forth the sheep by the thousands.

Psalm 144:13

That our garners *may be* full, affording all manner of store: *that* our sheep may bring forth thousands and ten thousands in our streets:

The original Hebrew word for thousand used in verse 13 is Strong's word #503, Alaph. Alaph means thousandfold. It is this verse of scripture that I base the thousandfold principle upon. David prayed for God to bring forth thousandfold and by ten thousands or a myriad. The thousandfold principle is replicated through the idea of multiplying by folding.

When farmers sow their seed into the ground they are expecting a bountiful harvest that is defined in folds.

Mark 4:20

And these are they which are sown on good ground; such as hear the word, and receive *it*, and bring forth fruit, some thirtyfold, some sixtyfold, and some an hundredfold.

Those that hear the word and receive it can bring forth fruit at thirty, sixty or even hundredfold levels. Folding is distinct from multiplying. When you multiply a number you are basically factoring it against the other number for a finite product. This is what we refer to in mathematics as a "Logical Axiom." A logical axiom is a self-evident truth, which is universally acceptable that is often taken for granted. For instance: $1 \times 1 = 1$ and $1 \times 2 = 2$. A statement such as, "supply equals demand" is an example of a logical axiom. No further explanation is necessary, because it explains itself.

Folding cannot be applied to a logical axiom. Folding is what is known as an "Illogical Axiom." An illogical axiom is a theory-dependent truth. In other words, in theory, if you have two apples with the same number of seeds in them, when planted they should yield the same number of trees. But we know that is likely not the case.

The seeds in one apple and the seeds in another apple may yield complete different results. So the equation is not obvious and cannot be controlled by a finite formula. In other words, you cannot simply say, "If I plant ten seeds from the apple it will yield a specific number." Each seed has a different potential and will develop according to its environment.

Farmers know that there will be a percentage of seed that will not reproduce because of the conditions around it. This is what the parable of the sower is all about. It is the soil, not the seed that changes. The seed never changes. It knows its assignment and it must reproduce after its own kind. It will not yield until it is released into its proper setting. Soil is the correct place for seed and good soil is the best place to plant it.

Once a seed has been sown into the ground, the soil takes over and begins to make the seed bring forth and bud. Sowing a persistent seed will result in a consistent harvest. Faith is what causes your seed to grow. The thirty, sixty and hundredfold yield is dependent upon the activation of your faith and the condition of the soil. If you give a money seed into a good ground ministry that is doing the work of the Kingdom of God, then it should yield in large measures.

Folding amounts to increase by doubling. Folding means to lay one part over another part by doubling, or to fold it over against itself. The first fold is the measure or standard for every fold thereafter and each time you double or fold you increase the material or substance exponentially, creating more rapid growth.

To put this in perspective, imagine you are holding a sheet by the corners and you fold the sheet so that the corners touch. Suppose that the area folded remains the same in size each time that it is folded. The first fold becomes the measure. Jesus said that the measure you give by would be the measure you live by.

Luke 6:38 NKJV
Give, and it will be given to you: good measure, pressed down, shaken together, and running over will be put into your bosom. For with the same measure that you use, it will be measured back to you.

Think about this, if you were to fold or double a sheet twenty one times, you would exceed the number one million! Each seed contains exponential ability to produce thousands upon thousands of seeds like itself, through the fruit that each seed creates.

3

For years I have believed in giving and receiving by the measure. I have learned through trust and experience that God multiplied my gift by folding the measure I gave by.

God does everything in the Kingdom by the measure. A measure is a standard unit used to express size, degree or the amount of something. Doing things by the measure makes things completely fair and equitable. Jesus taught us that we are to live, forgive, give, and receive by the measure.

God allots the measures that you need to fully function in the kingdom of God as a born-again believer. These measures are ample supply to achieve the purpose of each principle and gift in you. In the Kingdom of God everyone is given the same measure of faith.

Faith by measure
Romans 12:3b
God has dealt to every person the measure of faith.

Faith is what it takes to please God and faith is what it takes to exchange the promise and power of God from heaven to you. I like to say that faith is the ability to believe what God has said in His word. The measure of faith that God gives to you is the sufficient measure necessary to operate in the principles of the word to the full measure and potential.

The measure of faith you have is capable of believing and conceiving anything the word of God says is possible. All things are possible if you only believe by faith. Your faith is capable of operating at thirtyfold, sixtyfold or even hundredfold levels.

The hundredfold, being the highest of the three, is the fullest measure you can operate with in the earth.

The thousandfold is the unlimited measure and ability of God that is available to you through God's faith. The Apostle Paul wrote about the measure of faith given to everyone in Romans 12:3, but he also wrote about using God's faith as well.

Galatians 2:20
I am crucified with Christ: nevertheless I live; yet not I, but Christ lives in me: and the life which I now live in the flesh I live by **the faith of the Son of God**, who loved me, and gave himself for me.

When you are a Christian you are crucified with Christ, which means you are dead to the world but alive in Jesus. God gives you the measure of faith to believe His word and to trust in Him. Here Paul says that as a result of living the crucified life, he lives in the flesh, by the faith of the Son of God.

Your faith has the potential to function in the promises of God's word at full measure of the hundredfold. However there are times when you as a believer have the right and access to operate through the faith of Jesus. In other words, you can work the unlimited or thousandfold faith of the Son of God. The key to tapping into the thousandfold faith realm is to live the crucified life.

For 25 years my wife Darlene and I have trusted God with our life and our money. We knew that there were times where the $1,000 seed was what we needed to sow to see our situation turn around. It became an automatic reflex in us to give at thousand dollar levels. In fact, we decided that we would always obey God whenever we felt the unction to give $1,000 seed to an anointed vessel of ministry.

I have always been convinced by faith that sowing at thousand dollar levels was the will of God and that He honored the seed we sowed. Faith and trust in God's word has always been reason enough for me to do what I believe the word says and to follow the leading of the Holy Spirit.

The fact that the thousandfold principle works is sufficient in and of itself but I desired to know more about what caused the thousandfold to work. So I sought the Lord in fasting and prayer to discover the technical reasons why the number one thousand was so important in the Kingdom of God.

After years of study, prayer and supplications, God revealed this truth to me so that I could teach it to the Body of Christ. I know that there are many Christians that have acted in faith to give at thousandfold level and they have evidence of the miracle power of God to prove the thousandfold principle. This book should help Christians understand how the thousandfold principle works and how the entire Kingdom of God operates on the basis of the thousandfold.

The hundredfold is the full measure of return on a qualified seed. The thousandfold is God's unlimited ability to return on a qualified seed. The thousandfold is God's measure by which He operates. Thousand is the measure that God has chosen to build, support and balance His Kingdom and to transmit His power through.

Thousandfold is not an amount, it is a measure. It operates with exponential power similar to the way atomic power works. Atomic power is the result of the splitting of atoms that live a very, very long time. Atoms from a nuclear fission split and multiply at an exponential or extremely fast rate, creating vey high efficient energy. This causes a chain reaction to the atom increasing the number and accelerating the movement of the atoms.

I use this analogy because in my estimation, it mirrors the thousandfold principle. The thousandfold principle is like a nuclear response from the Holy Spirit of God in a chain reaction.

When the thousandfold principle is applied it causes things to grow and expand at extremely high rates causing incredible growth and maturity. The thousandfold principle causes things to move in your life at the speed of the Spirit, which is faster than any speed man can measure or describe.

The thousandfold principle is a force of power that works through faith and produces kingdom wisdom, anointing and power for the believer. The fruit of the thousandfold principle will generate miracles, signs, wonders and vast amounts of money for the Kingdom of God.

This book is the product of 25 years of instruction, impartation and experience of the thousandfold principle in action in my own life. The good news for you is that you can take hold of the thousandfold principle in much shorter order than I did.

This book was written so that you can learn how to tap into the unstoppable currents of the thousandfold flow of the eternal Kingdom of God now and forever. It was written so that you can understand the way that the thousandfold principle operates and to show you how God is using this principle in the last days for the end time harvest of souls and for all eternity.

Once you have completely read this book, you should begin to see the operation of the thousandfold principle throughout all of the pages of scripture. When you apply the thousandfold principle with faith and understanding, your life will forever be changed and empowered to see the invisible and do the impossible.

You will better understand why the number 1,000 is so important in the Kingdom of God. You will then be in a position to become a part of the end time army of Believers that will be used to finish the work of the preaching of the Gospel to all of the nations of the world and in the world to come.

Chapter 1

Thousandfold Miracles

Back Row Miracle

I love the word of God and have taught the Bible for over 25 years. As a young believer, I desired to learn the word and I get great satisfaction sharing the revelation that the Holy Spirit gives me with those who are hungry and thirsty for righteousness.

In my early years in ministry, I served at any capacity that I could in the church I was a member of. I was often asked by my pastors to fill in for them whenever they travelled. I was glad to oblige, but I will admit that I did not really know how to lead a congregation the way they did. However, I submitted to their requests and worked diligently to bring a timely message that would bless the people.

On one particular Sunday morning the house was filled to capacity with people. In the back row of the church there was a visiting family I had never seen before. It was a middle-aged couple that came with a newborn baby. The elders of the church came up and informed me that the family had a child that was on a heart monitor and that they needed prayer for the baby.

After the praise and worship team had finished, playing and singing, I stepped up to the pulpit to pray and speak to the congregation. We were flowing in the Spirit and the atmosphere was charged with expectancy. I began to exhort the people and encourage them about what I believed God was going to do that day. As I was talking I heard a high frequency squeal ringing in the room. At first I thought it was the sound system on the stage that was causing the feedback. I looked back to the sound booth to see what was wrong but they motioned to me that every thing was fine.

I then noticed that the family with the newborn was moving about as if something was wrong. Apparently the heart monitor on the child had gone off to warn the family that the child was in danger. I immediately instructed the ushers to bring the family forward with the intent of praying for the baby. The family brought the baby to the altar and as they were approaching towards me, the baby began to laugh and cackle loudly and the family began to sob and cry.

As the family began to walk down the middle of the isle carrying the baby with the heart monitor in fault, the Lord suddenly gave me an open vision above their heads. I saw the clouds of glory rolling back and the Lord Jesus sitting upon His throne with a child that looked like the baby they were carrying.

I did not want to say anything to them because I thought that this would scare them. I thought that God was saying that the baby was going to die, but he would be with the Lord and everything would be all right. I resisted saying anything about the vision but the Lord spoke to me and said, "Tell them what I am showing you."

I asked them if we had ever met or spoken before and they shook their heads no. I obeyed God and told the family exactly what God showed me in the open vision. The vision hovered over the family the whole time I was describing it to them. I told them that the baby on the lap of the Lord looked like the baby they were holding and then they wept profusely.

I did not know what to do at this point, I figured that I was delivering bad news to them and felt the best thing to do was let them take this moment in. The whole time the very tiny baby boy continued to move around, laugh and smile. I then asked the couple about the baby. They told me that the 5-month-old baby boy they held in their arms was their grandson and his name was Ernest. Ernest was wearing a heart monitor because he had a hole in his heart and they were instructed to bring him straight to the emergency room if the alarm went off.

Through their tears came forth smiles, laughter and expressions of hope as they proceeded to tell me that this was the first time that Ernest had responded like this and that he had never laughed or smiled from the day he was born. Everyone in the room shouted at the good news and rejoiced in the Lord with them.

It turns out that they were raising the child for the parents who were both in prison at the time. I was still thinking that the child in the vision was Ernest and that perhaps the Lord was telling them that the child would be in Heaven when that time came. I wanted to know if they were okay with these things that I shared about the baby on the lap of Jesus from the vision that remained above them.

The couple began to cry even harder than before and could not even speak. I was certain that I had missed God and should not have told them everything I saw, but the Lord affirmed again in me that I was doing the right thing by telling them everything I saw.

The aunt of the child was standing with them while all of this was happening and she spoke up on behalf of the grandparents. What the woman was about to say to me sent a shock wave of silence across the room that morning. She explained that Ernest was a twin of another baby boy that died after he was born.

The reason that they were so excited was because the vision confirmed what they had hoped for and believed. When she got done speaking the glory clouds folded back in towards the Lord on the throne and then disappeared. After hearing this great report the church erupted in shouts of praise and thanksgiving unto the Lord. We celebrated for some time as we all witnessed the miracle.

I was prompted by the Holy Spirit to receive an offering to honor the Lord right then and there. I instructed everyone to put money in his or her hands and place it in a basket and speak a blessing over it. I never saw so much money come into an offering so quickly. People were running to the altar praising and worshipping the Lord. They emptied their pockets out and gave in response to the miracle that day. The offering was the product of the people giving all that they could. This was truly a thousandfold miracle!

I found out 17 years later that Ernest had grown up into a healthy 17-year-old with a completely whole heart. God gave him a miracle! From that time forward I understood that there was a connection between the vision and the manifestation of the miracle through the offering we received that day. I believe that whenever God does something incredible, or whenever His word is performed, a gift sown into the Kingdom of God places a marker that cannot be erased or removed to memorialize the moment. This was the first time that God had used me to see an open vision like that but it was not the last time.

It is with this understanding that I apply the principle of sowing and reaping in miraculous situations such as this one. I have experienced the miraculous power of God at times where He performed notable and undeniable acts of His dunamis power, might and strength for healing, salvation, deliverance, and provisional prosperity miracles.

As time progressed I learned the secret of tapping into the unlimited, thousandfold power and anointing of God. I have experienced many, many miracles throughout the years and I detail in this book some of the more powerful miracles God gave to me. I hope that it will strengthen and encourage you to tap into the abundant flow of God's thousandfold Kingdom in your life!

I Shall Not Be Moved

As a believer in Jesus Christ I have learned how to trust God with the money He empowered me to earn, and to give into the Kingdom of God with purpose and desire. I fully understand the promise of seedtime and harvest as well as the principle of communicating in both giving and receiving in the Kingdom of God.

Over the years, my wife Darlene and I have progressively developed our faith in the various Biblical financial teachings through anointed men and women of God. When we first heard the teachings we were not quite sure if they applied to us or not but as we opened our ears to hear what the Spirit was saying to us through the word of God, we learned how to tap into these Biblical principles with measurable success. Biblical economics became a part of our daily life and we have never looked backed since.

I will never forget the first time I listened to brother John Avanzini on TBN talk about seed power. Up until this point I had never really considered how powerful a seed was. When I heard that brother John was coming to our hometown, I decided to go to the meetings and make every session.

In the first morning session I recall him saying these words in his slow, Texas draw, "Money is very spiritual." At first I was taken back by this comment, and a little bit offended. Just then the Holy Spirit told me to stay seated and listen because I needed to hear this. As John Avanzini began to share about the miracles that God had performed for his family I better understood the connection between the money he had given and the miracle God gave to his family and ministry.

My wife and I were embattled in a lawsuit to determine whether or not we got to stay in the house we bought under contract. The seller had allowed the insurance to lapse on the property, which put him in default on the mortgage that he held with the bank. This in turn created a problem for us. One thousand dollars is all the money that we had to our name and we needed this to move if we lost the court case.

A thousand dollars was a lot of money for us to give at that time and this would be the first time we had ever considered sowing at this level. After listening to the man of God teach on seedtime and harvest and other Biblical economic principles we decided to give to God more than we had ever done before. On the last night of the conference, we agreed to put a $1,000 seed in the offering as a testimony of the miracle we needed. I don't mind telling you that we felt like we had just given away the deed to our house but when the meeting was dismissed we gathered our stuff and headed towards the door.

I got in the car and I told my wife Darlene that the Holy Spirit just spoke to me and told me that we shall not be moved. We smiled at each other and drove away thinking about what we had just done. When we got home I walked to the end of the driveway and I held my hands in the air, and spoke to the house. I said, "We shall not be moved," and then I went back into the house and thanked God for the miracle I believed Him for.

The next day I was sharing about the problem with the house with a close friend on the telephone. I talked to him about the situation and then we hung up the phone. Fifteen minutes later he called me back. He said that he had talked to a realtor about the house and he wanted to look at it this afternoon if you are free, so I agreed. When the realtor came he asked me why we didn't sell the house and move to a new one. I told him that I did not know that we legally could. He explained that we had a right to put it up for sale and that we might as well after all what did we have to lose? So on his advice we signed a listing agreement the next day.

Before the for sale sign was placed in the front yard, the realtor called and wanted to show the house to a young couple engaged to be married. Later that night we got a phone call from the realtor because the couple wanted to make an offer. The offer not only cleared the legal battle out of the courts, it gave us the money for the down payment on our next home, and some extra cash. We knew that God had honored our $1,000 seed the night we gave it in the offering. God brought a buyer for the house, canceled the lawsuit, which paid off the house with money for a down payment on our next house, with several thousand dollars left over. God gave us the miracle and He returned the seed as well. Sometimes you get into situations and you feel powerless to do anything about it. God moved miraculously through the thousandfold principle and gave us a brand new start.

This would be the first of many opportunities to prove God in our giving, and to see God move miraculously on our behalf. We didn't always give a $1,000 seed in the offering, but there were numerous times that we felt that it were necessary. I would not recommend that anyone ever just try giving to God without understanding and expectation. It is imperative that you give and receive with faith and understanding. If you do not, you may likely become disappointed with the results. If you give with faith, patience and understanding, God is faithful and He will bring the harvest on the seed you sow when you are obedient to His voice.

Behind the Scenes

I have been in broadcasting all of my life. I grew up working in radio with my father. I started out working as the janitor and production assistant at the age of 11. I always dreamed about being a famous DJ on the radio. For 25 years God has given my family and me the opportunity to be the Trinity Broadcasting Network affiliate station in Louisville, Kentucky and Southern Indiana where we live. Back in 2002 the TBN Network announced a new youth network called JCTV. The network reaches young viewers 24-hours a day through music videos and other youth oriented programming. My son JJ works with me as my producer and editor for the station and my international program called Faith Now.

16

JJ was just 17-years-old at the time of the announcement about JCTV. God had given us a second TV station in the market to program and I was praying about what to do with the channel. JJ came to me and asked if we could become a JCTV affiliate. I agreed with him that if TBN would allow us to carry the new network that I would do it. TBN was glad to give us consent to transmit the network over the air on our second channel.

When Paul and Jan Crouch heard about my son's enthusiasm about the JCTV network, they decided to fly us out to California to be interviewed on the Behind the Scenes program. To say the least we were very excited about this opportunity. Apparently we were the first network affiliate station on the network.

On the way to the studios in Tustin, California we discussed what we would say during the interview. We also discussed sowing a $1,000 seed with TBN for the JCTV network as a seed for the equipment we needed to build the station in Louisville. I had taught the thousandfold principle to my family and JJ believed that it was the will of God to do this.

When we arrived at the TBN headquarters we toured the facilities and met some of the people that worked for TBN. Paul Crouch, Jr. hosted the program that day live at 5:00 PM PST.

We met Paul Jr. just a couple of minutes before the program went on the air, he is one of the most pleasant and diplomatic men I have ever met. This was the first time we had met him and we did not talk to him about our project or the $1,000 seed.

We came on during the second segment of the program to talk about the station affiliation. Neither Paul Crouch, Jr. nor anyone at the network knew anything about our plans to give $1,000 to JCTV prior to the interview. We did not even know if it was proper etiquette to do this or not. Paul Jr. asked us some questions about the station and our ministry. We presented a Louisville Slugger baseball bat with his dad's signature on it and then we told him that we had a gift for JCTV. JJ briefly shared about the thousandfold principle and then handed Paul Jr. the $1,000 check.

What we did not know was that Paul and Jan Crouch were watching at their home and had instructed their assistant at TBN to deliver a message from them for Paul Jr. to read on the air. Paul Jr. received this message from his parents and the check from JJ on the set at the same time. The fax read that Paul Jr. was to tell us that Paul and Jan were personally going to give us $10,000 for our station project. Paul Jr. smiled and said, "I don't think this has ever happened in the history of the TBN network, this is a spiritual lesson taking place right in front of our very eyes." Before we could tell them what we wanted to do God had multiplied the seed ten times. God caused the harvest to overtake the seed sown.

Amos 9:13
Behold, the days come, says the LORD, that the plowman shall overtake the reaper, and the treader of grapes him that sows seed; and the mountains shall drop sweet wine, and all the hills shall melt.

The thousandfold principle was fast at work. God moved quickly on the seed and produced the harvest we needed. Paul Jr. immediately took us into Paul Sr.'s office and gave us a personal check from Paul and Jan Crouch. The greatest thing

18

about this thousandfold money miracle was the fact there were millions of people watching this take place live on TV. It was a true testimony of God's ability to multiply the seed sown that day. That thousandfold seed has kept the JCTV network on the air in Louisville, Kentucky until this day.

I have posted the video of the Behind the Scenes program on my website www.johnwsmithjr.com for review. It will verify and document this thousandfold miracle.

The MS Miracle

In 1998, I began to feel very dizzy and disoriented and I became very forgetful. My limbs would twitch for no reason at all. One afternoon while I was in a store with my wife and youngest daughter, I lost my balance and then suddenly fell down knocking over an isle display. I got up from the floor and told my wife Darlene that I thought it was time to see a doctor.

Several weeks later I was in my car on the way to the office, during rush hour traffic, when suddenly my legs and arms went numb. I could barely control the steering wheel and I was unable to move my legs to step on the brake. At first I panicked thinking that I may crash.

I managed to get the cell phone in my hand and hit the speed dial for my wife Darlene. When she answered I told her what was going on and that I needed her to pray for me to arrive safely out of traffic. I told her that I wanted her to know what was going on in case I was in an accident. She prayed for me and I was able to get to the emergency room for treatment.

19

I was barely able to make it from the car to the emergency room. I was exhausted and then fell to the floor unable to pick myself up. The nurses quickly ran to my aid and put me in a wheelchair to take me in the examination room to run tests. They took x-rays and ran a CT scan on me. Everything pointed to the signs of Multiple Sclerosis better known as MS.

The doctor then checked my vital signs and asked some questions about how I was feeling and what was going on with me. I explained what had begun to happen to me over the past several weeks. After performing some tests and examining me, he then recommended that I see a neurologist for further testing.

Upon hearing the prognosis of the doctor, I decided to sow a $1,000 seed as a testimony of my faith in God's word that I was healed by the stripes that Jesus took upon His back. I still felt the symptoms and things seemed to get progressively worse, but I kept my confession and kept on praising the Lord.

I went to the neurologists and he conducted a brainwave test. I remember being in a dark room with a strobe light flashing. They had connected probes to my head so that they could read the brain wave activity. After reviewing the results of the brainwave, the doctor felt that I needed to have an MRI to see in detail what my brain looked like.

When I went for the MRI at the local hospital, I put on headphones to block out the clicking noise in the MRI chamber. As the magnet moved around and took pictures of my brain, I confessed scripture out loud. I confessed Psalm 103 over and over again, believing that healing was my God-given benefit and that God had delivered me from this affliction.

About a week went by, and it was time to visit the neurologist for a follow up on the MRI. My wife and I went into the waiting room and took a seat with other patients that could barely sign in or even walk. I began to cry as I saw what these people had to go through to perform basic tasks.

Thank God for my precious wife Darlene. When she saw my reaction to the other patients, she grabbed my hand and whispered in my ear, "You have a beautiful brain." I thought that was an odd thing to say, but I received her words and her warm smile.

Fifteen minutes later they called my wife and I back to see the neurologist for the reading of the MRI results. He told me a little bit about how the MRI worked and then showed us 31 separate pictures of my brain taken at different angles. The doctor took each picture and explained what they revealed and at times traced his finger over the image describing what was going on in my head. I will never forget what he said when he lifted the last picture in front of the shadow box.

He pointed at the image of the arteries and the veins in my neck and said they were clear. He then pointed to the image of the crown of my brain and then he lifted his index finger and smiled while saying, "Mr. Smith, you have a beautiful brain." These words were exactly the same words my wife had spoken in my ear just fifteen minutes earlier!

There was no question that God had answered my prayer and honored my $1,000 seed. The Bible says that in the mouth of two or three witnesses, everything is established. Because both my wife and the doctor said that I had a beautiful brain, I believe that God was telling me that I would not have to live with multiple sclerosis and that He had honored my faith and my $1,000 seed sown.

I left the doctors office rejoicing over the good report. I still felt the symptoms in my body for over three months, but I continued to thank God for the confirmation of His miracle power every day. After the three months had passed, I no longer felt the symptoms and a final check up with the neurologist gave me a clean bill of health.

Every day of my life I thank God for what He did for me and I am reminded that there was a direct connection between my seed of $1,000 sown in faith and the miracle deliverance from MS.

I believe that God will honor every seed sown in faith. God is not a respecter of persons; He is a respecter of principles. God does not perform His word in your life because you need Him to, He performs His word in your life because you want Him to. The seed you sow is evidence that you believe He can and that He will perform His word for you.

My $1,000 seed was my evidence that I trusted God for His anointing and dunamis power to breakthrough and destroy the problem. I believe that giving to God documents your faith and declares the testimony of your miracle. The thousandfold seed serves as a memorial mark; it places a stay on your situation, which can prevent it from coming into your life again.

My Grandson Miracle

At the age of 46, the thing I wanted more than anything in my life was a grandchild. On January 1, 2009 my son's wife went to the emergency room with a terrible headache. My wife called to let me know and to pray for her. I asked her to notify me when they were released from the emergency room so I could come by and visit with them.

When I arrived at the ministry office that afternoon, they told me that my daughter-in-law was pregnant and expecting in September 2009. I was so excited I jumped around the room rejoicing in the good news. From that moment on, I told everyone that I met that I was going to be a Grandpa.

When the time came for the ultrasound tests on the baby, we expected a good report from the doctor. However, the report from the doctor was not good. The doctors said that they believed from the results of the tests that the baby had a high possibility of being born with downs syndrome and cystic fibrosis.

I think that people that have downs syndrome are some of the most precious people I have ever known. So if you know someone who has downs syndrome, please do not take this as a negative comment against him or her, it is the disease I have an issue with, not the people.

We coupled our faith with a $1,000 seed for the purpose of testifying that we believed the report of the Lord over the report of the world. So we gave the $1,000 seed as quickly as we could into a covenant ministry. Then the Holy Spirit led us to give several $1,000 seeds on our grandson's behalf. We sowed the seed, prayed and agreed together in Jesus name that the baby was going to be perfect.

Medical technology has come a long way from when my wife and I had our three children. They now have MRI and ultrasound equipment that can give you a detailed, 3D preview of what the baby looks like in the womb. We were looking forward to seeing a three dimensional ultrasound of the precious baby in his mother's womb.

We gathered with our family and my daughter-in-law's family to see the image of the child on a projected video screen. The baby boy kept his hands over his face, preventing a clear view of the bridge of his nose. Everyone was somewhat disappointed, but I made the remark that I believed that it was the glory of God in the womb that made him to cover his face. The doctors were looking for evidence on the bridge of his little nose to confirm the downs syndrome diagnosis. I was looking for the prefect face of a beautiful baby boy.

We came a week later to see the three dimensional image, but he still would not move his hands away from his face. We believed we would see the evidence of our confession that he was whole and had no downs syndrome or any other affliction, others were looking for evidence of downs syndrome. My family knew that God had honored our $1,000 seed sown as a testimony of the baby being what we said, that he was perfect. Every day my wife and I agreed in prayer that the baby was completely whole and that he was perfect.

On September 9, 2009, or 9-9-09, Isaiah Carter Smith was born without a trace of downs syndrome or any other ailment, including cystic fibrosis. That afternoon Carter came into the world and was handed to my son and his wife. The nurses and all that saw him that day said, "He is Perfect." The confession we made when we sowed the $1,000 seed became the report of everyone about Isaiah Carter Smith. He was and he is still perfect, praise God!

Shawn's Miracle

Just before I wrote this book I spent a couple of weeks teaching my congregation about the thousandfold principle. When I finished the series I challenged the people to sow a $1,000 seed based on their faith and understanding of the teaching. Many of them did and there were a number of great things that happened as a result of the seeds sown.

One of the women in the church had been battling cervical cancer for a while and we prayed for her to receive her healing. On the same Sunday that I challenged the people to give the $1,000 seed, she reported that the doctors had given her a clean bill of health and that the cancer was gone! She and her husband gave their first $1,000 seed that morning. We rejoiced with the family and gave God all the praise.

The very next week I got a frantic phone call from the woman who was healed of cancer. She was on her way to meet her mother-in-law in Indianapolis, Indiana to pick up one of her sons, named Shawn. Shawn had spent the week with his grandparents in Champaign, Illinois. Shawn and his grandmother were on Highway 40 East when suddenly the car hit a blown truck tire in the middle of the road. The car flipped five times and landed on its roof with Shawn hanging out of the window.

By the grace of God there was a state policeman and an ambulance driver that witnessed the accident in traffic. They rushed Shawn and his grandma to the hospital for emergency treatment. My wife and I prayed for Shawn and his grandmother and immediately took authority over the spirit of death. We drove straight to Champaign that night to minister to the entire family. We arrived at around 3:00 AM and went to the hospital room to lay hands on Shawn.

We came into the room and found Shawn and his father in the room. Shawn's dad fell into my arms and began to sob profusely. Shawn was unconscious with scrapes and bruises on his body. He had a broken collarbone and an extreme head trauma. The doctors told the parents that it did not look good. The doctors said that Shawn's brain had separated from the impact and that it would take a long time to recover and that he would have the mental capacity of a kindergartener. I encouraged Shawn's dad that God was going to get the glory in this matter and that Shawn was going to fully recover.

We stayed in the hospital room and prayed for Shawn while his parents attended to other things. In less than 12 hours Shawn woke up and spoke. In less than 24 hours Shawn was flown back home by helicopter like his parents wanted. Within three days Shawn was recovering fast and celebrated his eighth birthday that week. Shawn's grandmother was discharged from the hospital a couple of days after the accident and she has fully recovered.

The $1,000 seed that was given to my ministry by this family became the thousandfold seed that protected and restored Shawn and his grandma. The thousandfold seed produced a miracle that defied the doctor's reports in less than 24-hours. Today Shawn is back in school fully recovered and attending church with his family.

Thousandfold Miracle for You

Every one of these miracles was associated with the $1,000 seed sown as a testimony of the power of the thousandfold principle. The seed you sow should always be accompanied with a good confession of what you want and what you believe. I believe that it is very important that you establish what you want and what you believe by making the confession at the moment you give to God.

The seed does not buy miracles it serves as a testimony of the miracle and as evidence to the people. Essentially your seed sown produces a voice that speaks to God to create a sacrifice that He can accept. Your seed puts the problem on notice that it is no longer permitted in your life, and more importantly, it gives glory to God!

These are some of the most distinctive thousandfold miracles we have seen take place in our life since we took hold of the thousandfold principle, but they are not the only ones. God has honored this seedtime and harvest principle on a regular basis for me. There is a specific reason that I sow in thousand dollar levels. That is the subject of this teaching. I pray that you will listen with your heart and ask the Holy Spirit to reveal this powerful Kingdom principle to you as he did to me.

Let me add this extremely important point, my wife and I are practicing tithers. We consistently bring the tithes and offerings into the storehouse where we worship God every week. We do not steal from God and expect Him to bless a thief. The thousand-fold principle will not work if you are not in proper covenant with God in the tithes and offerings.

I decided to document these miracles in the first chapter to build your faith in the thousandfold principle. You will discover that the thousandfold principle works in conjunction with the $1,000 seed, but you will learn so much more. It is my prayer that those who see and understand the thousandfold principle will act upon it in faith and witness the powerful force of the thousandfold, unlimited God that we serve.

I encourage you to keep a journal of the progress that takes place when you receive your thousandfold miracle. Please feel free to submit your miracle reports to me so we can rejoice with you.

Chapter 2
Testimony of a Gift

In order to determine the thousandfold principle you must understand why giving to God is relevant to moving God into your situations. All throughout the Bible we see examples of people making sacrifices to God whenever they needed to hear from Him, or after they had an encounter with Him.

Presenting a gift to God has always been standard practice when approaching Him on a matter or request. Many of the people in the Bible gave freewill offerings to God to show their appreciation for God's power and presence. Others gave to fulfill what the word of God required. In the New Testament Jesus was met by a leper who desired cleansing from his disease. Here we find an example of how a gift given obediently into the Kingdom of God will bring the witness of a miracle.

Matthew 8:1-4
When he was come down from the mountain, great multitudes followed him. [2]And, behold, there came a leper and worshipped him, saying, Lord, if you will, you can make me clean. [3]And Jesus put forth *his* hand, and touched him, saying, I will; be you clean. And immediately his leprosy was cleansed. [4]And Jesus said unto him, See you tell no man; but go your way, show yourself to the priest, and offer the gift that Moses commanded, for a testimony unto them.

Jesus came down from the mountain where he was praying, when a leper came and worshipped Him and said that he believed that it was the will of God to cleanse him. Jesus

29

touched the leper and said to "be clean." There are a couple of things you can learn from this encounter.

First, your worship must say something. The leper presented his confession through his worship. Worshipping God from the heart presents your words before the Lord. Worship corrects your focus on the Lord and opens up the pathway to exchange with Him as the High Priest of your confession.

Upon receiving the miracle Jesus instructed the leper to present the offering to the Priest as a testimony of his faith in God. This was the right thing to do according to the Law of Moses and it was the right thing to do according to the instructions that Jesus gave to him. The offering was tangible evidence that was given as a memorial, or a reminder, to God that the person giving was healed or made whole by God's word. It served as a confirmation of God's word.

You do not have to wait for the manifestation of a miracle to confirm your faith in God. You can sow seed in advance to demonstrate that you believe that God is faithful to complete the miracle by His Spirit and through His word.

When you sow a seed in advance you are saying to God that you trust in Him with all of your heart and that you believe that God's word is confirmed in your life and situation. This applies to anything that you desire to come to pass in your life that is consistent with the promises of God that are all yes and amen in Christ Jesus!

Believers should always connect their giving with a confession. In the book of Deuteronomy Chapter 26, the word of God required that the people of God were to have a priest, a place, and a profession for their gifts that they presented in sacrifice to the Lord. When the people brought their gift to the Priest they made a good confession over the offering before the Lord.

Deuteronomy 26:9-10
And he has brought us into this place, and has given us this land, *even* a land that flows with milk and honey. [10]And now, behold, I have brought the firstfruits of the land, which you, O LORD, have given me. And you shall set it before the LORD your God, and worship before the LORD your God.

The Israelites had a specific confession that stated they were no longer enslaved or in bondage to the past, and that the gift they were offering was evidence of their confession. Christians should do the same thing when they give to God today. Your words empower God to release His promise and power in your life. Your confession makes a statement of faith that marks where you are and where you are going from that point on. Believers should always have a good confession over all of the gifts that they give to God, including their tithes and offerings.

The Israelites brought their tithes, offerings, first fruits and sacrificial seeds to the priest who received their gifts in a basket. The Priest then spoke a blessing over the offering and over the people. The Israelites came to the house of God and placed their gifts in a basket that would be waved by the Priest before God. This is vastly different than today's traditional method of giving to God.

31

I personally believe that it is very important to pray over every offering before giving it to God. When a man or woman of God speaks a blessing over your offering it releases the blessing and empowerment of God over your entire life. In Ezekiel Chapter 44 God declares that the people should bring their first fruits offerings to the Priest so that they could pronounce a blessing over their household.

Ezekiel 44:30
And the first of all the firstfruits of all *things*, and every oblation of all, of every *sort* of your oblations, shall be the priest's: you shall also give unto the priest the first of your dough, that he may cause the blessing to rest in your house.

The people of God were told to bring the first fruits of all of their offerings to the Priest so that they may cause a blessing to rest upon their household. This is not widely accepted today but the word of God does not change and so this principle is still current.

Jesus spoke a blessing over the offering of the five loaves and the two fish in the wilderness. This offering was then multiplied by the thousandfold as a result of the prayer of thanksgiving that Jesus prayed. I pray over all the gifts that come into our ministry and I speak the thousandfold blessing over the gift and the giver.

Passing the plate is an indifferent and cold way of giving to God. I am not sure where this tradition came from, but I don't see any evidence of this practice in scripture. Passing the plate around sends out a message that God is coming to you for help, this is completely backwards. Coming to God demonstrates our humility and recognition that we need His help.

Many people lack understanding on how giving and receiving works in the kingdom of God. Unfortunately some Christians think that when they give to a church or ministry organization it is just for paying the bills. Although the money should be used for the budget of the church or ministry, that is not the main reason that we give. There are a number of reasons why we give to God.

- To learn to respect and love the Lord always.
- To demonstrate that He gives us the power to get wealth.
- To open Heaven and shut down Hell.
- To be a blessing to the church and to those in need.

Others understand giving but lack understanding about receiving. Giving is only half of the promise of God for you. You must learn to be a receiver as well.

Nothing is more important in giving and receiving than having the right attitude. The way you approach God when you give is just as important as giving in the correct measure. When Israel presented their sacrifices to God they came with praise and worship as they brought the sacrifice to the Priest. They knew that the sacrificial gift in their hands represented the blessing and covenant of God in their life. They came singing and praising the Lord in celebration of what God had done for them.

Psalm 100
Make a joyful noise unto the LORD, all you lands. [2]Serve the LORD with gladness: come before his presence with singing. [3]Know you that the LORD he *is* God: *it is* he *that* has made us, and not we ourselves; *we are* his people, and the sheep of his pasture. [4]Enter into his gates with thanksgiving, *and* into his

courts with praise: be thankful unto him, *and* bless his name.
⁵For the LORD *is* good; his mercy *is* everlasting; and his truth *endures* to all generations.

The people sang this song every time they came to the Tabernacle or the Temple. If they did not bring the gift with joy and thanksgiving, then their gift would not be accepted. Remember, God loves a cheerful giver whose heart is in their giving. Your gifts must come from the heart and then through the hand. That means you must let go of the gift internally before you give it externally.

For example, God accepted and approved Abel's sacrifice, but rejected Cain's. God accepted the gifts from those who had sold land and laid them at the Apostles' feet in the book of Acts. God rejected the gifts from Ananias and Sapphira because they lied to Peter about the amount of money. Cain's attitude resulted in a curse on his life and both Ananias and Sapphira died on the spot for lying to the Holy Ghost.

God keeps a close watch on how much you give and how you give. In the book of Mark Chapter 12, Jesus remarked about a widow that gave two mites in the offering.

Mark 12:41-44
And Jesus sat over against the treasury, and beheld how the people cast money into the treasury: and many that were rich cast in much. ⁴²And there came a certain poor widow, and she threw in two mites, which make a farthing. ⁴³And he called *unto him* his disciples, and said unto them, Verily I say unto you, That this poor widow has cast more in, than all they which have cast into the treasury: ⁴⁴For all *they* did cast in of their abundance; but she of her want did cast in all that she had, *even* all her living.

Jesus said that she had given more than all the rich people had given collectively. Jesus knew how much the rich gave but the widow's seed got His attention. Jesus made it a point to speak out loud to His disciples on the very moment that she gave. He essentially said that her seed carried more power than the combined offering of all the rich people who gave.

Jesus said that she gave of her want and that she had cast in all of her living. He knew that this money was everything that she had in the world and that she had given from her extreme poverty, with a purpose. The widow decided that she was done living at the same day-to-day level and to change her present state and condition of living by throwing everything she could into the kingdom.

We can only imagine what level she went to since her seed sown was larger by measure than the entire offering! I explain in Chapter 9 how this kind of giving is qualified as a thousandfold seed.

The widow's mites spoke to the Lord. Her seed qualified her for an incredible return and as a result, the Lord compared the gifts of the rich to her seed. A seed must be qualified before it can be multiplied. A qualified seed is one that is acceptable by God and gains the respect of God. The widow's two mites did both. She gained the respect of Jesus and a financial abundance from the seed sown.

Once you sow a qualified seed in the Kingdom of God, then God will multiply your seed according to the measure you gave by. He will also increase the fruits of you righteousness as well. This amounts to the true riches of the Kingdom of God, such as the anointing. The attitude you have when you give to God shows the level of respect you have for Him. The amount or measure shows the level of love that you have towards Him. The first recorded offering in the Bible is found in the Old Testament book of Genesis. Adam and Eve had two sons that both brought an offering to God, but God approved only one of them.

Genesis 4:3-5

And in process of time it came to pass, that Cain brought of the fruit of the ground an offering unto the LORD. [4]And Abel, he also brought of the firstlings of his flock and of the fat thereof. And the LORD had respect unto Abel and to his offering: [5]But unto Cain and to his offering he had not respect. And Cain was very wroth, and his countenance fell.

Hebrews 11:4

By faith Abel offered unto God a more excellent sacrifice than Cain, by which he obtained witness that he was righteous, God testifying of his gifts: and by it he being dead yet speaks.

Abel presented an acceptable, or more excellent, sacrifice to God than Cain did because he gave the first of his flocks, and because he gave with the right countenance. Cain did not present an acceptable offering. What he gave to God was not his first and it was not his best.

Some people think that Cain's offering was not accepted by God because it was not a blood sacrifice, but that is simply not so. The reason that God rejected Cain's offering was because it did not satisfy the requirements of the first fruits giving and because he did not give by faith. Faith is the element necessary to please God. Without faith it is impossible to please Him.

Hebrews 11:6
But without faith *it is* impossible to please *him*: for he that comes to God must believe that he is, and *that* he is a rewarder of them that diligently seek him.

God knew that Abel was a shepherd and He also knew that Cain was a farmer. Certainly God would not have expected Cain to bring livestock or herds for the sacrifice when his resources came from the field. So Cain's offering failed to meet the criteria with God because it was not the first and best of his crops.

Abel's gift to God was qualified because it came from his heart and it was his first and his best. Abel gave with the proper understanding and attitude. Abel's gift is called a more excellent sacrifice. Excellent is the Greek word, Pleon, which means larger in quantity and better in quality. From this we can deduce that comparatively Abel's gift was a much larger portion and of a much higher quality.

Cain's heart was not right before God, nor was the order, measure or quality of his offering. This kind of giving will never require God to accept your gift and can in fact bring detrimental results. Abel gave to God by faith. Faith works by love. So therefore, Abel loved to give to God and it empowered his faith in his offering. Abel's more excellent sacrifice did three specific things:

- Bore witness of his righteousness.
- Produced testimony from God of his gifts.
- Gave voice to his faith that speaks beyond the grave.

When you give from your heart with faith and understanding it will produce the same things in your life. Your gift can literally transcend time itself and speak many years beyond your life on this planet.

When the woman with the alabaster box of ointment came to pour the anointing oil on the body of Jesus it caused a sweet smelling aroma to fill the house for everyone to partake of; but those who were in the room that were indignant did not get to enjoy its benefits.

Mark 14:3-11

And being in Bethany in the house of Simon the leper, as he sat at meat, there came a woman having an alabaster box of ointment of spikenard very precious; and she brake the box, and poured *it* on his head. [4]And there were some that had indignation within themselves, and said, Why was this waste of the ointment made? [5]For it might have been sold for more than three hundred pence, and have been given to the poor. And they murmured against her. [6]And Jesus said, Let her alone; why trouble you her? she has wrought a good work on me. [7]For you have the poor with you always, and when so ever you will you may do them good: but me you have not always. [8]She has done what she could: she is come afore hand to anoint my body to the burying. [9]Verily I say unto you, where so ever this gospel shall be preached throughout the whole world, *this* also that she has done shall be spoken of for a memorial of her. [10]And Judas Iscariot, one of the twelve, went unto the chief priests, to betray him unto them. [11]And when they heard *it*, they were glad, and promised to give him money. And he sought how he might conveniently betray him.

This alabaster box of anointing oil was worth over a year's wages. Just like the widow with the two mites, she tapped into the thousandfold principle by giving all that she had. In verse 8, Jesus said she had done what she could. In other words, she took everything she had to bring the gift to pour upon Jesus. It was valued at 300 pence. This would equate to a year's wages in those days. Imagine sowing an entire year's salary in one single offering. The only thing that would compel you to do this would be the gratitude for what God has done for your life.

The New Living Translation says that the people in the house scolded her harshly. Jesus understood the real issue. It was not that they had a problem with her giving that much money, but that they had a problem with her giving that much money to God. Remember, those who became indignant did not recognize Jesus as the Son of God, they saw Him as the carpenter's son from Nazareth, Mary's boy. This prevented them from seeing the importance of sowing into an anointed vessel of God.

This woman's gift of anointing perfume was honored by Jesus as a memorial offering in preparation of His death, burial and resurrection. Memorial giving marks the moment of faith in which you sowed a significant seed in the kingdom of God. A significant seed is one that moves you towards God and God towards you. Memorial giving activates the covenant of God for you and it brings Him into remembrance of His promise to bless you.

The woman with the alabaster box of perfume broke the container that held the perfume. Her desire was to connect with Jesus through the gift and to pour her most precious possession upon His life. Notice that she had to break the box first before she could pour the perfume on the Lord. Why not just open it?

In order for you to go to another level, you are going to have to go outside the containment of your present situation. In the box, the oil was in an unresponsive state. It could not do anymore than be held in place. The oil was not designed to be stationary, it was designed to flow and as long as the alabaster box was wrapped and sealed around it, it could not fulfill its purpose.

Because she chose to break the box she would never be able to resort to the containment of her past again! When the oil touched Jesus, the value of the oil increased. Every gift that is given into the Kingdom of God is poured on the Lord and it will increase in value. The money you give to God will go from a finite value in this world to an infinite value that is out of this world!

Judas Iscariot thought the oil should be sold and the money given to the poor, which would have limited the value of the gift to the market value. Judas knew the immediate value to be three hundred pence but he did not know the eternal value of the box. A pence is a metal coin that was probably made of gold or silver. The Greek word for Pence is Denarion, which is equal in value to ten donkeys.

If it were a year's wages in today's age it could have been worth $50,000 to $100,000. If the oil were sold that is all that it could have ever become. After she poured the oil on the Lord, the value of the perfume became priceless. The woman's alabaster box of ointment served as a testimony of her faith and of the Gospel of Jesus Christ. When you give a gift in the same fashion as this woman did, your gift will become a reminder before God as a testimony of your faith.

Sometimes a gift is given to the Lord as a testimony for the recovery of lost things and the discovery of the unknown. In the Old Testament book of 1st Samuel Chapter 9 there is a story about the lost donkeys of a man named Kish. Kish was from the tribe of Benjamin and he was the father of Saul. Saul was sent by his father to go look for the lost donkeys. Saul took a servant with him and began to search for them.

1 Samuel 9:6-10

And he said unto him, Behold now, *there is* in this city a man of God, and *he is* an honorable man; all that he says comes surely to pass: now let us go thither; peradventure he can show us our way that we should go. [7]Then said Saul to his servant, But, behold, *if* we go, what shall we bring the man? for the bread is spent in our vessels, and *there is* not a present to bring to the man of God: what have we? [8]And the servant answered Saul again, and said, Behold, I have here at hand the fourth part of a shekel of silver: *that* will I give to the man of God, to tell us our way. [9](Beforetime in Israel, when a man went to enquire of God, thus he spoke, Come, and let us go to the seer: for *he that is* now *called* a Prophet was beforetime called a Seer.) [10]Then said Saul to his servant, Well said; come, let us go. So they went unto the city where the man of God *was*.

Saul's servant knew that the prophet Samuel was honorable and that the way to honor him was to bring a gift to him. Saul did not have anything to give the man of God but the servant did. So they pursued the prophet with a sacrificial seed in hand so that they could find the lost donkeys of Kish.

41

This servant had given everything that he had to honor the prophet on behalf of his master. Whenever you give in this fashion you are tapping into the thousandfold realm. The servant's seed would secure the lost donkeys and serve to be the starting point of the kings over the nation of Israel.

1 Samuel 9:15-17
Now the LORD had told Samuel in his ear a day before Saul came, saying, [16]To morrow about this time I will send you a man out of the land of Benjamin, and you shall anoint him *to be* captain over my people Israel, that he may save my people out of the hand of the Philistines: for I have looked upon my people, because their cry is come unto me. [17]And when Samuel saw Saul, the LORD said unto him, Behold the man whom I spoke to you of! this same shall reign over my people.

1 Samuel 9:20
And as for your donkeys that were lost three days ago, set not your mind on them; for they are found. And on whom *is* all the desire of Israel? *Is it* not on you, and on your father's house?

The servant's gift was given to Samuel to honor him as the prophet and to get his wisdom on Kish's lost donkeys. By the time that Saul and his servant arrived in town, the donkeys have already been found. They came into town with the hopes of recovering something that was lost and they left town discovering something they did not know.

The seed of the servant was like a two-edged sword. On the one hand it was the mechanism that brought back the donkeys, on the other hand it was the catalyst that released the anointing upon Saul to be the first King of Israel. A simple servant's seed helped pave the way to establish the throne over the entire

Kingdom of God. This means that a forth part of a shekel of silver would become the thousandfold seed of the Kingdom of God on the earth.

This is true of Jesus as well. His God-given mission was to seek and save that which was lost. His sacrifice on the cross of Calvary was the ultimate thousandfold seed. He is the living testimony of the seed that God promised in the Garden of Eden. As a result of His death, burial and resurrection the entire human race can come back to the Heavenly Father. Jesus gave His life for the sins of the whole world so that you could have the abundant, overflowing life that He experienced before time existed.

Jesus is the ultimate thousandfold seed. He is the unlimited measure of God's Spirit, anointing and love for those who believe in Him. The purpose of this chapter is to show you how that sacrificial gifts presented to God will make a mark that cannot be removed as a memorial before Him. This is a fundamental principle that establishes how the thousandfold principle works. All of the remaining chapters to follow are based upon the concept of the testimony of a gift that invokes the presence of God.

Thousandfold Principle

Chapter 3
Thousandfold Kingdom

Psalm 90:12
So teach us to number our days, that we may apply our hearts unto wisdom.

Moses wrote the 90th Psalm. He knew that there was a connection between numbers and our life. He knew that the numbers corresponded to the wisdom of God as well. The Holy Spirit teaches us the significance of the value of numbers and letters as they are written in the original text of the scriptures so that we can draw wisdom from them.

Numbers have a very significant function in relation to the way that God speaks to you in the Bible. They accomplish specific tasks to measure out time needed to complete something and other certain instructions that will produce a manifestation of His glory.

God's Kingdom is divinely ordered by His word. Everything in creation was made by the spoken word of God and it is the sound of those words that produced the substance and matter we see and hear around us. God has a specific purpose in mind whenever He instructs you to do something a certain number of times, or in exact amounts of money to be given. If you refuse God's instructions you are rejecting God's authority and the blessing that comes with obedience.

Often times the things that God instructed people to do in the Bible did not make any natural sense. However, upon execution of obedience to a prophetic word from the Lord they found out that God had a plan to bless them for obeying Him. Many times that inspired instruction came with a numeric assignment attached to it. God always has a reason for the specific number instruction He gives. The instruction is often associated with the core meaning of the number itself.

For instance, God told Joshua, the captain of the hosts of Israel, that He had given Jericho, its king and all the men of valor to him. God gave a very detailed numeric instruction to Joshua that would bring this promise to pass.

Joshua 6:3-4
And you shall compass the city, all *you* men of war, *and* go round about the city once. This shall you do six days. ⁴And seven priests shall bear before the ark seven trumpets of rams' horns: and the seventh day you shall compass the city seven times, and the priests shall blow with the trumpets.

When the people of God obey God and do things exactly the number of times that He tells them to, then God will perform His word accordingly. There is no magical element to the numbers in and of themselves. The primary purpose for numbers is to create order. Order brings the manifestation of provision, protection and power to your life.

Without order, chaos will emerge and destroy your life. Numbers help arrange the system of order by which we do things and they produce a particular behavioral pattern that maintains that system of order. We all function properly on a numeric schedule. When we get off schedule problems develop and cause us pain. Pain is the product of disorder. This is true in your body, relationships and money. The way to deal with pain is to treat the disorder. The treatment for every disorder will have a numeric instruction. The doctor will prescribe that you take a medication a certain number of times in a day to deal with the pain caused by the disorder. If you want pain to go away, the disorder must be rearranged and balanced so that order can return and the pain can leave.

Numbers serve a significant function in the natural flow of things and in the realm of the spirit. Numbers are used to create rhythm and harmony between two or more parties. Numbers produce a standard that we can all operate by and agree with. Numbers are used to bring definition and agreement to everything that exists. In the mouth of two or three witnesses everything is established. The power of agreement is a numeric principle.

If you use your faith and obey the inspired numeric instructions of an anointed vessel, it will produce miraculous results. For example, there was a man named Naaman who was the chief captain of the armies of Syria. He was a great and honorable man but he was a leper. In his quest for healing he goes to see the prophet Elisha.

2 Kings 5:9-13

So Naaman came with his horses and with his chariot, and stood at the door of the house of Elisha. [10]And Elisha sent a messenger unto him, saying, *Go and wash in Jordan seven times, and your flesh shall come again to you, and you shall be clean.* [11]But Naaman was wroth, and went away, and said, Behold, I thought, He will surely come out to me, and stand, and call on the name of the LORD his God, and strike his hand over the place, and recover the leper. [12]*Are* not Abana and Pharpar, rivers of Damascus, better than all the waters of Israel? may I not wash in them, and be clean? So he turned and went away in a rage.

[13]And his servants came near, and spoke unto him, and said, my father, *if* the prophet had told you *to do some* great thing, would you not have done *it*? How much rather then, when he said to you, Wash, and be clean?

Naaman the leper was told to wash seven times in the river Jordan to be cleansed. Elisha did not tell him dip until you feel healed, he told him to dip exactly seven times. Naaman did not like the instruction because he did not like the location where he was to dip. He wanted a better river to dip in seven times. He was insulted that Elisha did not come out to meet him. He wanted to control the environment for the miracle instead of obeying the prophet Elisha and receiving his miracle. It did not make sense to Naaman to wash his unclean flesh in an unclean river. In his mind a clean river would produce clean flesh.

If it had not been for his servants, Naaman probably would not have gone to the Jordan River and followed the instructions of the man of God. He most likely would have gone away complaining about how the preacher is always trying to tell you what to do. The servants had more faith in the instruction than Naaman did. It is good to have people of faith around you that have your best interest at heart. Naaman must have respected his servants' opinion and so he followed the instructions to dip seven times in the Jordan River.

2 Kings 5:14
Then went he down, and *dipped himself seven times in Jordan, according to the saying of the man of God*: and his flesh came again like unto the flesh of a little child, and he was clean.

Why seven times? The number seven in Hebrew is the word pronounced Sheba. It comes from the root word that means to complete or swear for an oath. Elisha had Naaman dip seven times to complete an oath. Obedience to do what the man of God said gave Naaman his miracle.

When you follow through with the inspired instructions given to you, God will bless and reward you for being faithful to His word. It may not always make sense to you and in fact it seldom will, but the miraculous often comes through the ridiculous. Giving a specific amount of money as a seed in the Kingdom of God will bring wisdom and miracle power in your situation.

Many of the numbers in the Bible correspond to a specific definition and meaning. When the meaning of the number is applied to the text of scripture, it extracts the revelation of the passage for deeper learning and understanding.

Here is a list of numbers and their spiritual meaning:

1=Unity
2=Agreement
3=Trinity
4=Power
5=Grace
6=Man
7=Rest
8=New Beginnings
9=Spirit
10-Completion
12-Government
20-Redemption
40-Season

50-Freedom
100- Fullness
400- Divine Separation
666-Number of the Anti-Christ
1000-Limitless

Beyond the relation between numbers and their meanings that are recorded in the Bible, there is a hidden message embedded and encoded within the words and letters of the text of scripture. This hidden system of numbering letters and assigning meanings to them is called Gematria. Gematria comes from the word geometry.

The Gematria of the original Hebrew and Greek alphabet spell out hidden messages and meanings as a subtext to the written word. The Gematria helps us better understand the full purpose and meaning of the word of God. We will deal more in detail with the subject of Gematria later in this book.

God has created all things by His spoken word. That means that everything that exists is a product of sound.

Genesis 1:1
In the beginning God created the heaven and the earth.
John 1:1-3
In the beginning was the Word, and the Word was with God, and the Word was God. [2]The same was in the beginning with God. [3]All things were made by him; and without him was not any thing made that was made.
Colossians 1:16-17
For by him were all things created, that are in heaven, and that are in earth, visible and invisible, whether they be thrones, or dominions, or principalities, or powers: all things were created

by him, and for him: [17]And he is before all things, and by him all things consist.

Mankind is also a product of the spoken word and the breath of the Holy Spirit. So man is a direct result of the reverberation of the mouth of God. In Him we live and move and have our being.

Acts 17:28
For in him we live, and move, and have our being; as certain also of your own poets have said, for we are also his offspring.

Man is an intelligent, mathematical design that is built on a numeric code known as DNA, which is short for deoxyribonucleic acid. DNA contains the information that creates the schematic of our physical and spiritual existence.

The information in DNA is stored as a code made up of four chemical bases: adenine (A), guanine (G), cytosine (C), and thymine (T). Human DNA consists of about 3 billion bases, and more than 99 percent of those bases are the same in all people.

The order, or sequence, of these bases determines the information available for building and maintaining our body, spirit and soul, similar to the way in which letters of the alphabet appear in a certain order to form words and sentences. The DNA in you maps out a number that corresponds directly to the sound of the word of God that is spoken into you.

When the word of God is spoken it writes a mathematic sentence or equation. It inscribes a numeric code that is self-replicating, which means that it can reproduce after its own kind like a seed does. This presents one of the greatest supporting evidences to creation. In order for any number to be entered into an equation, such as the numeric code of DNA, there must be an intelligent force to insert the number. It makes absolutely no sense that the structure of all creation just happened to fall in place by some arbitrary cataclysmic event like the theory of evolution suggests.

God is a super intelligent mathematic genius that made the foundation of creation on the base of a number system. It is by this number system that God manufactured the heavens, the earth and everything that exists.

Words are subject to interpretation, but numbers never lie. Ask your accountant and they will tell you the same thing. Whether it is an equation or a balance sheet, the numbers on them will always give the same answers. When God created the heaven and the earth He did so by speaking. Whatever God spoke, He saw. What He saw was the manifestation of the words He spoke that encoded the numbers in us that produce the sum total of our genetics.

The genetic code creates a number base system that can be identified and counted by medical science and by God the creator. So all of creation has a number base counting system upon which it is built. It is the foundation for the building blocks of life. The Bible says that we are fearfully and wonderfully made. Everything was made with a precise numeric value. God has an accurate record that has an exact count of every fiber in you.

Luke 12:7a
But even the very hairs of your head are all numbered.

God is a God of integrity and accuracy. Everything in creation is word-made and therefore has a number that registers its existence. Jesus gives us insight to the fact that God stamps a serial number on the individual hairs on our body. The verse doesn't say that God just keeps track of the total number of the hairs we have but that our entire being is numbered, the same way that Ford Motor Company numbers the parts of an automobile on the assembly line with a serial number.

Every vehicle manufactured has the same parts as the others made in the same line, but every part has a unique digit assigned to identify it. This helps the owner of the car to communicate with the manufacturer when a replacement part is needed. The Kingdom of God operates with the same principal. When you believe God for healing and restoration of your triune being, He has the replacement parts you need.

The word of God is the warranty that authorizes you to make a claim with Him. Faith is the documentation of your belief in the warranty that God will honor. When you confess the word of God it will restore, reconcile and replenish the things that have been missing, broken or stolen.

In mathematics we use "base numbers systems" for formulas and equations. There are various base number systems used for different purposes such as the base six systems, which was introduced to American schools in the 1970's. The base six system uses the number symbols 0 through 5 in each digit rather than 0 through 9. Base six identifies that there are five-fingers on each hand and it asserts that this is a more natural way of counting. The NCAA collegiate sports rules use base six to identify the jersey numbers of the players. This is to make it easier for a referee official to use their fingers to make calls.

There is the base two system which is used for binary code in digital data signals for cell phones, computers and other digital based electronics. The binary number system uses ones and zeroes in varied sequences to represent other numbers. The ones and zeroes act as off and on switches that keep information precise and flowing.

The binary code for the number 1000 actually looks like this: 1111101000. The numbers we typically count are in decimal form such as 1,2,3,4,5,6...and so on. Decimal form numbers can be converted into binary numbers. The binary number 1000 is the decimal number 8. The number 8 is the number for new beginnings. The interesting thing about the number 1000 is that when you reach the count of 1000 you have to start over again. So the number 8 and 1000 function much the same.

The base ten system is the most widely accepted system of decimal notation in modern society. The tithe is the tenth of all the increase God brings into your life. The Bible instructs all Christians to return the tithe back to God so that He may bless you. God and Abraham established the tithe after the battle of the kings in the valley of Shaveh.

Abraham defeated all of the wicked kings and brought back all of their spoils. When Abraham met Melchizedek on the road, Abraham exchanged one tenth of all of the spoils he gained from war for the communion bread and wine in the hands of the High Priest.

Abraham was the first person to do this and therefore established the tithe as the portion that belongs to God. That is what established the first tenth of all your increase as the portion you give to God when you fellowship with the Lord.

The whole Kingdom of God operates on the thousand base systems. There are 521 times that the word thousand is used in scripture. God uses thousand as the basis of building and maturing. God measures by thousands, counts by thousands and builds his Kingdom on the foundation of a thousandfold structure.

One thousand is the number that relates to the operation and infrastructure of the Kingdom of God. When stating His position of prosperity on the earth, God says that the number one thousand upholds His prosperity.

Psalm 50:10
For every beast of the forest *is* mine, *and* the cattle upon a thousand hills.

The thousand hills in Psalm 50 are representative of the foundation of prosperity. In other words, the thousand hills are what support the cattle on them. So a thousand is used for the base system of prosperity in the Kingdom of God. Certainly there are many more than a thousand hills on the planet, but here God chooses to define His ownership of the planet in measures of one thousand.

When God counts, He counts differently than you do. God counts and measures by the thousands. When you start a count you usually begin with the number one. When God counts He begins with the number 1000. In the Kingdom of God one and one thousand are the same to Him.

55

2 Peter 3:8

But, beloved, be not ignorant of this one thing, that one day *is* with the Lord as a thousand years, and a thousand years as one day.

Isaiah 60:22

A little one shall become a thousand, and a small one a strong nation: I the LORD will hasten it in his time.

In the mind of God there is no difference between one and one thousand. The number one and the number one thousand are essentially the same to Him. We count one, two, three, four etc...but when God counts He counts 1000, 2000, 3000 etc...

God counts by the thousands and He measures by the thousands. If you were to use a measuring tape it would be marked in increments by inches and centimeters. If God were to pull out His measuring device, it would be marked in increments of one thousand.

Ezekiel 47:3-5

And when the man that had the line in his hand went forth eastward, he measured a thousand cubits, and he brought me through the waters; the waters *were* to the ankles. ⁴Again he measured a thousand, and brought me through the waters; the waters *were* to the knees. Again he measured a thousand, and brought me through; the waters *were* to the loins. ⁵Afterward he measured a thousand; *and it was* a river that I could not pass over: for the waters were risen, waters to swim in, a river that could not be passed over.

Ezekiel saw this vision of the man with the measuring line in His hand. This is of course the Lord that He sees quantifying the size of the Temple. This Temple known as Ezekiel's Temple is actually the eternal Temple of God with the unlimited flow of the Holy Spirit coming forth from doorways of the Temple.

The man measures one thousand four times. The number four is the number of the Divine Creation of the Holy Spirit.

Here are some examples of the Divine use of four:

- 4 Elements: Earth, Wind, Fire, Water.
- 4 Regions: North, South, East, West.
- 4 Divisions of time: Morning, Noon, Evening, Midnight.
- 4 Seasons: Spring, Summer, Autumn, Winter.
- 4 Rivers in Eden: Pison, Gihon, Hiddekel, Euphrates.

The Temple of God overflows with unlimited power, presence, promise and peace in the vision. The four, one thousand measures produced waters to swim in. This is the unlimited thousandfold flow of the water of life that comes from the Holy Spirit.

When the Church recognizes the thousandfold principle as the foundational principle of the Kingdom of God, we will swim in the unlimited thousandfold power of the Kingdom of God!

The Kingdom of God is a thousandfold kingdom because the Kingdom of God is unlimited. The thousandfold is the unlimited measure of God's power and ability. Solomon was given the throne of his father King David as the newly anointed king of the nation of Israel.

Solomon is still a young man and he does not have the experience or wisdom to rule as a king. So he decides that he must meet with God to obtain the wisdom necessary to handle the assignment responsibly.

Solomon gets the revelation that offering exactly one thousand animals in sacrifice is the amount needed to intersect with God so that he can reign and rule with wisdom and understanding.

1 Kings 3:4-5
And the king went to Gibeon to sacrifice there; for that *was* the great high place: a thousand burnt offerings did Solomon offer upon that altar. [5]In Gibeon the LORD appeared to Solomon in a dream by night: and God said, Ask what I shall give you.

Solomon knew that in order to get God's attention he would need to make a sacrifice of monumental proportions. Solomon brings exactly one thousand animals as an offering to God. After Solomon finished the thousandfold sacrifice, he went to sleep. God came to Solomon in a dream granting what he wanted from Him. Solomon made his request to God and God gave him the desire of his heart.

1 Kings 3:9-13
Give therefore your servant an understanding heart to judge your people, that I may discern between good and bad: for who is able to judge so great a people? [10]And the speech pleased the Lord, that Solomon had asked this thing. [11]And God said unto him, Because you have asked this thing, and have not asked for yourself long life; neither have asked riches for yourself, nor have asked the life of your enemies; but have asked for yourself understanding to discern judgment;

[12]Behold, I have done according to your words: lo, I have given you a wise and an understanding heart; so that there was none like you before you, neither after you shall any arise like unto you. [13]And I have also given you that which you have not asked, both riches, and honor: so that there shall not be any among the kings like unto you all your days.

Solomon's prayer was accompanied by his 1000 sacrificial animal offerings. Here you see the importance of sowing a seed with your prayers. They mix together as a memorial before God. Now that Solomon has received the answer to his prayers and more, he is prepared to begin reigning and ruling as a king.

The wisdom of God gave Solomon immense wealth, great favor and blessing to rule the people and to build the Temple. The wisdom of God made Solomon a great communicator and negotiator. His communication skills helped him in conjunction with the building of the Temple. Solomon applied the wisdom that God gave to him in two areas. First, the wisdom of God magnetically attracted people towards him for counsel, which in turn they gave him super abundance of wealth and riches. Second, he was skilled in the art of negotiation, which empowered him to bring the finest materials for the Temple building.

Solomon built four different houses during his lifetime:

- The Temple.
- His own house.
- The house in the Forest of Lebanon.
- His wives' house.

Solomon used the wisdom of God to make the connections to bring in the supplies to build the Temple. His alliance with King Hiram produced the cedar and fir trees that he desired. Solomon repaid Hiram with twenty thousand measures of wheat every year during the seven-year construction project.

The thousandfold principle worked through Solomon's life in many areas, including the exchanges in his business affairs. From this point on Solomon begins to bring forth things from his life by multiples of thousands.

1 Kings 4:32
And he spoke three thousand proverbs: and his songs were a thousand and five.

Solomon's intellectual property of poems and songs were all counted by multiples of thousands. The thousandfold principle projected from within his spirit into the things that he spoke and wrote. Imagine what the royalties would pay an author or songwriter today for that many works.

I believe that every Christian should be compensated for the things that they produce from their spirit. Many well-known believers today are blessed financially by every word and thought that proceeds from them. Some carry the same anointing that Solomon carried in the area of music and the arts. God's people should reproduce and dominate by multiples of thousands in seven areas including:

- Finance
- Business
- Education
- Politics
- Arts
- Media
- Science

Everything that Solomon touched produced in measures of thousands. After finishing the Temple, which took seven years to complete, Solomon again offered sacrifices to God in thousandfold multiples.

1 Kings 8:63
And Solomon offered a sacrifice of peace offerings, which he offered unto the LORD, two and twenty thousand oxen, and an hundred and twenty thousand sheep. So the king and all the children of Israel dedicated the house of the LORD.

Solomon's wealth had increased over seven years to the point he could offer a total of 142,000 animal sacrifices. Again his hand is releasing in multiples of one thousand. His seed before God is now 142 times bigger than when he began seven years earlier. God pronounced the blessing of favor, honor, riches, and life through the thousandfold sacrifice Solomon gave at Gibeon. God had blessed Solomon immensely as he said that he would.

The thousandfold principle has increased Solomon to the place where he can basically write a check for whatever his heart desires. Isn't that where you long to be as well? You can get there if you take hold of this principle and apply diligence to see God enter into your dreams and grant you all the favor and wisdom needed to achieve them!

Solomon's understanding of the thousandfold created a new set of problems for him. Not the type of problems you may think; good problems.

1 Kings 8:63-64
And Solomon offered a sacrifice of peace offerings, which he offered unto the LORD, two and twenty thousand oxen, and an

hundred and twenty thousand sheep. So the king and all the children of Israel dedicated the house of the LORD. [64]The same day did the king hallow the middle of the court that *was* before the house of the LORD: for there he offered burnt offerings, and meat offerings, and the fat of the peace offerings: because the brasen altar that *was* before the LORD *was* too little to receive the burnt offerings, and meat offerings, and the fat of the peace offerings.

The only problem that Solomon had was that the altar was not large enough for his gift. How would you like for your greatest issue to be that the place where you give is not big enough for your offerings? The solution to the problem for Solomon was to declare the entire outer court from the altar to the porch steps of the Temple to be holy ground. When Solomon did this it not only made more room for his gift, it enlarged the territory of God's holiness in his life. So in fact his gift made room for him before God.

Proverbs 18:16
A man's gift makes room for him, and brings him before great men.

Solomon's gift sent an invitation for God to meet with him and discuss his heart's desires. God came to Solomon again in 1 Kings Chapter 9 to let Solomon know that He had heard and received his prayer and his sacrificial gift. Again this is Solomon's prayer coupled with an offering based on the thousandfold principle.

Solomon set the standard for the thousandfold kingdom by sowing a thousandfold seed. If you can receive this, a thousandfold seed is a "King size seed." The thousandfold seed that Solomon sowed established the throne of the king in Israel. The Apostle Paul said that we are presently seated with Jesus in heavenly places. I believe that when you give with thousandfold purpose and understanding that it declares your position with Jesus Christ as a king that rules with Him.

The thousandfold kingdom is an unlimited, unstoppable force of power and anointing that you can tap into today. Jesus taught us to pray for God's Kingdom to come on earth as it is in Heaven. This is one of the ways that you can release the Kingdom of God with all of its power and authority in the world now. The Kingdom of God is within you, sow the thousandfold seed and take dominion over everything that moves!

Chapter 4
Thousandfold Blessing

A paradigm is a pattern or model for something. The thousandfold principle is a paradigm in the kingdom of God. A paradigm establishes the method and pattern of how something works universally. Gravity is a universal paradigm for successful science. Gravity is not a theory; it is a proven fact that applies to the entire planet and all of its contents. The thousandfold principle is a Kingdom paradigm that is used as a successful method of building, developing and supporting the entire Kingdom of God. It is the model on which the unlimited power and resources of God are based.

Whenever you study the word of God you must build your faith and understanding upon a foundational principle as the standard of what you believe in. Everything in the word of God is line upon line and precept upon precept. That means that anything you read in the scriptures should line up and agree with all other scriptures in its complete context. This is what makes the word of God infallible. It always agrees with itself.

The first mention of something in the Bible establishes the principle, or paradigm, throughout the entire scope of all scripture. For instance, Abraham was the first to present the tithe to God in the book of Genesis. The tithe, or tenth, became the amount that we exchange with God off the top of all our increase that honors Him as the High Priest of our confession. There are many other Kingdom paradigms that work for us including faith. Faith was first mentioned through Abraham and therefore he is known as the father of us all in faith. The thousandfold principle was first mentioned through Abraham's life too.

Genesis 20:1-3

And Abraham journeyed from there toward the south country, and dwelled between Kadesh and Shur, and sojourned in Gerar. ²And Abraham said of Sarah his wife, She *is* my sister: and Abimelech king of Gerar sent, and took Sarah. ³But God came to Abimelech in a dream by night, and said to him, Behold, you *are but* a dead man, for the woman which you have taken; for she *is* a man's wife.

Abraham's wife Sarah must have been a beautiful woman to look at because Abraham was afraid that the heathen nations they travelled through might kill him and take Sarah from him. Abraham told the people of Gerar that Sarah was his sister. He did this to protect their lives and to protect the promise God gave to him concerning his and Sarah's future. This was not a lie, it was the truth. Sarah was his half sister on his father's side, which made it acceptable for him to marry her.

Abimelech placed Sarah in his harem but did not touch her. When Abimelech went to sleep that night, God came to warn him in a dream not to touch her or he would die. Abimelech protested that he had not touched her and that he would not have done this thing on purpose. He was a moral and upright man and he was a man of integrity. God let him know that He prevented this thing from happening because of His righteousness. Abimelech was then warned by God not to touch her.

Genesis 20:3

But God came to Abimelech in a dream by night, and said to him, Behold, you *are but* a dead man, for the woman which you have taken; for she *is* a man's wife.

Genesis 20:4-7

But Abimelech had not come near her: and he said, Lord, will you slay also a righteous nation? *5*Said he not unto me, She *is* my sister? and she, even she herself said, He *is* my brother: in the integrity of my heart and innocency of my hands have I done this. *6*And God said unto him in a dream, Yes, I know that you did this in the integrity of your heart; for I also withheld you from sinning against me: therefore suffered I you not to touch her. *7*Now therefore restore the man *his* wife; for he *is* a prophet, and he shall pray for you, and you shall live: and if you restore *her* not, know you that you shall surely die, you, and all that *are* yours.

God agrees that Abimelech was innocent, however ignorance is no excuse when you are in danger. God came to Abimelech through His grace to warn Abimelech of impending doom for his entire household. Touching a man or woman of God through their family can be just as hazardous to your health as touching them directly.

You don't have to physically touch someone to harm them. When you talk about, gossip or verbally assault a person you will inflict as much or more damage than if you struck them physically. God does not take these things lightly, because when you assault the vessel you are assaulting the anointing upon them and God will not allow you to get away with that.

Psalm 105:14-15

He suffered no man to do them wrong: yes, he reproved kings for their sakes; [15]*Saying*, Touch not mine anointed, and do my prophets no harm.

Perhaps Abimelech was just looking for someone who could conceive children with him? No one in his family was able to bring forth children and apparently he was eager to have children in his household. Abimelech took heed to the warning from God in the dream and he placed honor on Abraham by giving him livestock, servants and land. He also gave Abraham one thousand pieces of silver for his error.

Genesis 20:14-16

And Abimelech took sheep, and oxen, and menservants, and women servants, and gave *them* unto Abraham, and restored him Sarah his wife. [15]And Abimelech said, Behold, my land *is* before you: dwell where it pleases you. [16]And unto Sarah he said, Behold, I have given your brother a thousand *pieces* of silver: behold, he *is* to you a covering of the eyes, unto all that *are* with you, and with all *other*: thus she was reproved.

Abimelech gave Abraham one thousand pieces of silver to honor Sarah for her innocency in the matter and to justify any claim against her. Silver is the metal of redemption in the Bible. The thousand pieces of silver represent the redemption of Sarah's life.

The thousand pieces of silver that Abimelech gave to Abraham tapped into the thousandfold principle, which saved his life and the lives of his entire household. This goes to show you that the thousandfold principle can act on the behalf of others as an intercession for their lives. Now Abraham can speak as a prophet for Abimelech and everyone in his house in prayer to God.

Genesis 20:17-18
So Abraham prayed unto God: and God healed Abimelech, and his wife, and his maidservants; and they bare *children*. [18]For the LORD had fast closed up all the wombs of the house of Abimelech, because of Sarah Abraham's wife.

Before Abimelech gave the one thousand pieces of silver to Abraham, God would not permit the household of Abimelech to bear children. In order for the Abimelech household to conceive children they would all need a healing from God. When Abimelech honored Abraham with the thousandfold gift of one thousand pieces of silver, it caused the prayers of Abraham to release the healing anointing upon the entire household.

The one thousand pieces of silver brought God into the situation and He honored the prayers of his faithful friend Abraham on behalf of Abimelech. You may wonder why God didn't just heal Abimelech without the intercession of Abraham? God always works through an anointed man or woman of God in the five-fold ministry to release His anointing for a miracle.

Finding an anointed man or woman of God to sow a significant seed through can open up the floodgate of fruitfulness in your life. This is an important element in making the anointing connection that will heal you and bless you as well. Abimelech must have instinctively known that one thousand pieces of silver was the right amount to give in this particular situation. The one thousand pieces of silver stopped death in its tracks and it produced new life for his entire household. This seed opened up the wombs of the women to conceive. The thousandfold seed can open a natural womb and the womb of your spirit to create new opportunities, new ideas and new life.

Allow me to explain how it works. God created the heaven and the earth and then put man in it to be fruitful, to multiply and to replenish it. God gave the dominion over the earth to Adam male and Adam female. The word dominion is a compound word that means king's domain. The dominion given to Adam essentially transferred God's rights and authority over what happened on the planet. The dominion empowered Adam to declare what was allowable and what was not allowable. All permissions to move on the planet earth came through Adam.

The earth still belongs to God, the world and the inhabitants of it. Adam became the Governor of the earth who would exercise kingdom law over every being and situation. Notice that God made Adam male and female. The two of them were one before God and when God called for Adam both of them would respond. Adam female came from Adam male and was given to Adam male as a helper. She was not to usurp his authority and he was not to lord it over her. Both of them had the God-given rights to rule over the planet but they had to respect the divine order God set up. God told Adam and his wife to take dominion over three realms including land, air and sea.

Genesis 1:27-28

So God created man in his *own* image, in the image of God created he him; male and female created he them. [28]And God blessed them, and God said unto them, Be fruitful, and multiply, and replenish the earth, and subdue it: and have dominion over the fish of the sea, and over the fowl of the air, and over every living thing that moves upon the earth.

God does not and will not usurp the authority He gave to mankind. He only intervenes when the will of man allows him to. Many folks say God is in control. This is true only to the degree that man opens up their will and invites Him to be involved. That is why God gave you faith. Faith opens and invites God to move on your behalf.

This is a very important principal to understand. God does not arbitrarily do things on a whim. Although He is sovereign in His power and nature, He does not impose His sovereignty upon mankind. He wants to perform His will in your life and He will do so according to the operation of your faith. Some people believe that if God wants something to happen that He will just do it. God moves through your faith in Him. Contrary to popular belief, God does not prove His will, you prove His will.

Romans 12:2

And be not conformed to this world: but be you transformed by the renewing of your mind, that you may prove what *is* that good, and acceptable, and perfect, will of God.

Again, whenever something is first mentioned in scripture it establishes the standard from that point on. God needs a human being to open a door on earth so that He can open the door of Heaven and legally enter into the world through man's will. God will not violate His agreement with mankind concerning the dominion given to him in the beginning. This is what Jesus explains to you in John's Gospel.

John 10:1-2

Verily, verily, I say unto you, He that enters not by the door into the sheepfold, but climbs up some other way, the same is a thief and a robber. [2]But he that enters in by the door is the shepherd of the sheep.

The only legal door into the earth is through the womb of a woman. The devil came into the Garden of Eden and stole the dominion and blessing from Adam and bypassed the legal entry into the world. He came through an animal, not a man. The devil came another way and took the dominion that was handed over to him by Adam. Jesus came legally and lawfully to destroy the works of the devil and to return the dominion back to man through His redeeming blood.

Galatians 4:4-5

But when the fullness of the time was come, God sent forth his Son, made of a woman, made under the law, [5]To redeem them that were under the law, that we might receive the adoption of sons.

Jesus was able to come through the door of a woman's womb and become the sacrifice for the sins of all mankind because people opened doors on the earth to make it legal for God to return the favor. For instance, God asked Abraham to offer Isaac in sacrifice to Him. Isaac was Abraham's son of promise. Abraham agreed to do this and because of his willingness to lay Isaac on the wood altar, God stopped Abraham before he plunged the knife into Isaac's body. As a result of this first step on the earth to give the first son of promise, it opened the door for God to give Jesus as His only begotten son as a sacrifice for the sins of the whole world.

There are a number of first mentions in the Bible that opened the door of heaven and established the Kingdom principles we operate through. As we have examined in this chapter, the thousandfold principle was first mentioned in Genesis Chapter 20. From that point on the gift of one thousand would become the measure that would qualify as the amount that would garner God's attention. The thousandfold principle acts as a type of key that unlocks things in the spirit realm.

When God delivered Israel from the bondage of Egypt, He intended for them to go straight into the promise land. They refused to believe God's word and consequently did not enter into the land flowing with milk and honey. God kept them and sustained them for forty years in the wilderness even though they refused to believe Him. Moses was the deliverer that God sent to free the nation from four hundred years of slavery. In the wilderness Moses spoke a blessing to the people.

Deuteronomy 1:11
The LORD God of your fathers make you a thousand times so many more as you *are*, and bless you, as he has promised you!

Moses spoke the thousandfold blessing over the nation of former slaves. These people started out as a small, meager group of souls that were held captive and forced to work in the labor camps of the Pharaoh. God prophesied this event in a dream to Abraham hundreds of years prior to this occasion. The Bible says that the more that the Egyptians afflicted the

Hebrews, the greater they grew. Affliction and persecution always serve a greater purpose. They will make you increase and strengthen.

God told Abraham that even though the people would be enslaved by a foreign nation, they would come out with great substance. They all came out with silver and gold and there were no sick or feeble among them. They walked out of Egypt with abundant wealth. Now these people are standing in the wilderness as a multitude of stars in number. They have grown from a handful of slaves into a force to be reckoned with. Now Moses is speaking the thousandfold blessing over them to increase them as the stars of the heavens.

You must also consistently confess the thousandfold blessing over your life so that the unlimited power of God will come upon you. The thousandfold blessing is transferred by the spoken word of God from generation to generation.

Deuteronomy 7:9
Know therefore that the LORD your God, he *is* God, the faithful God, which keeps covenant and mercy with them that love him and keep his commandments to a thousand generations;

The thousandfold blessing is a powerful force that transcends time and penetrates the ages with energy and might that transforms any situation or circumstance. Each time the thousandfold blessing is transferred from one generation to the next, it increases exponentially in thousandfold measure.

A generation is typically a span of twenty-five years or so. According to this verse of scripture God extends His covenant to those who love Him for a period of up to 25,000 years. We have just crossed over 6,000 years in this age. This promise demonstrates that God is willing to go way beyond our needs! The promise to keep the covenant to a thousand generations is a thousandfold promise to all of God's people.

God's covenant with you is a covenant of prosperity and health that will cause you to be fruitful and multiply without limits. The thousandfold blessing causes things to multiply by the thousands. One of the most notable thousandfold miracle in the New Testament is the story of the feeding of the five thousand families in the desert.

John 6:1-7

After these things Jesus went over the sea of Galilee, which is *the sea* of Tiberias. [2]And a great multitude followed him, because they saw his miracles which he did on them that were diseased. [3]And Jesus went up into a mountain, and there he sat with his disciples. [4]And the passover, a feast of the Jews, was nigh. [5]When Jesus then lifted up *his* eyes, and saw a great company come unto him, he said unto Philip, When shall we buy bread, that these may eat? [6]And this he said to prove him: for he himself knew what he would do. [7]Philip answered him, Two hundred pennyworth of bread is not sufficient for them, that every one of them may take a little.

The multitudes followed Jesus into the wilderness and they had stood for three days in the desert listening to Jesus teach. The people are hungry and Jesus does not want to send them away fasting. He knows exactly what He can do to take care of the situation but he wants to prove the principle to the disciples.

We don't know a lot about the disciple Philip, but we can see that Philip has an insufficiency mentality. You know the type, there never seems to be enough and nothing will work because they can't see how there is enough to go around. Jesus knew that Philip had an insufficient mentality and He wanted to prove to Philip that little can become much in the hands of the Lord. You cannot improve until you are first proven.

Philip didn't understand how the equivalent of forty dollars would purchase enough bread for the massive crowd of five thousand families. The 5,000 is referring to the number of men in the crowd because in that day they did not number the women and children. So the actual size of the crowd was perhaps as many as 30,000. It was a lot of people to feed no matter how you slice the bread. The number 5,000 is significant as this miracle multiplies through the thousandfold blessing.

The disciple Andrew located the lad who brought the five loaves of bread and the two fish that would become the seed for the thousandfold miracle. Andrew had a gift of bringing people to Jesus. He brought his brother Simon Peter to the Lord and he found this little boy.

John 6:8-10
One of his disciples, Andrew, Simon Peter's brother, said unto him, [9]There is a lad here, which has five barley loaves, and two small fishes: but what are they among so many? [10]And Jesus said, Make the men sit down. Now there was much grass in the place. So the men sat down, in number about five thousand.
(Note: Verse 10 says about five thousand, however the number is confirmed by Jesus as five thousand men in Matthew 16:9)

Jesus told the disciples to make the 5,000 men sit down. The crowd had been standing on their feet for three days because they were in a desert place and there was nowhere to sit until they did what the disciples told them to do; sit down.

Verse 10 says, "Now there was much grass in the place"...miraculously the desert place produced a blanket of plush grass.

The desert is a dangerous place to be in during the daytime and at night. Psalm 23 says that the Lord makes me lie down in green grass and He prepares a table for me in the presence of my enemies. The green grass is known as the tablelands, which are the plush and abundant ground where sheep are led to feed by good shepherds. Obedience is critical to the manifestation of the word of God for you.

You may not like the instructions or corrections of a spiritual mentor but you will reap the rewards of their words. When you listen and obey, the difficult places will become easy.

Jesus received the loaves and the fish from the lad and then handed the pieces to the disciples. The disciples and the crowd became distributors of the miracle as they watched the seed grow before their very eyes.

John 6:11
And Jesus took the loaves; and when he had given thanks, he distributed to the disciples, and the disciples to them that were set down; and likewise of the fishes as much as they would.

If Jesus wanted to He could have commanded the stones of the field to be made bread. In Luke Chapter 4 Jesus was challenged by satan in the wilderness to command the stones to be made bread. The devil did not question whether or not Jesus could perform the miracle; in fact satan knew that Jesus could. The truth is that satan wasn't questioning Jesus ability, he was questioning Jesus identity. The devil questioned and said, "If you are the son of God?" Jesus did not need to do a miracle to prove who He was. He knew who He was and He knew what He could do.

Everyone got to partake in the thousandfold miracle and everyone had a hand in the thousandfold blessing that multiplied the food. The disciples who did not think that they had enough to meet the demand gathered up the fragments that remained in twelve full baskets. The word remained is the Greek word Per-is-syoo-o which means super abounding. The overflow of the thousandfold miracle produced a super abundance of supply. If the remains are called super abundance, what is the portion that they came from called? Answer, thousandfold.

John 6:12-14

When they were filled, he said unto his disciples, gather up the fragments that remain, that nothing be lost. [13]Therefore they gathered *them* together, and filled twelve baskets with the fragments of the five barley loaves, which remained over and above unto them that had eaten. [14]Then those men, when they had seen the miracle that Jesus did, said, this is of a truth that prophet that should come into the world.

The twelve baskets would rightfully belong to the little boy. God gives seed to the sower and bread to the eater, so the only problem the boy had that day was how to transport the twelve baskets. Jesus worked that problem out for the boy by having the disciples gather and carry them for him. The twelve baskets full of fragments were not just the little boy's harvest on the seed he had sown, it was also his thousandfold seed to do whatever he wanted to with it.

The reason that this miracle reproduced in thousandfold force is because the five loaves and two fish functioned as a thousandfold seed for the little boy. The five loaves and two fish amounted to everything the boy had. The thousandfold miracle took affect because the boy gave everything he had. In essence the five loaves and the two fish had the same power as one thousand loaves and one thousand fish would carry. The five loaves that the little boy gave to Jesus in John Chapter 6 became the meal for five thousand men and their households. If you divide the five loaves into the five thousand people you get the number one thousand. The power of the thousandfold multiplied the bread and the fish.

The twelve baskets of bread fragments came from the original five loaves of bread. In the natural order of things bread is the harvest of a seed sown. However anything you give to the Lord will act as a seed. So the bread fragments can either be eaten or sown. Twelve baskets full of anything is a lot to deal with. Twelve baskets full of bread is certainly more bread than one person can digest. Bread has a short shelf life and bread back then was only good for a week or so. Giving the bread to others will serve a greater purpose and it will perpetuate the blessing of the thousandfold principle.

This was not the only time that this provisional miracle of the loaves and the fish occurred in Jesus ministry. In fact, this provisional miracle became the standard protocol for feeding the masses.

The thousandfold blessing worked consistently for Jesus and His disciples. Although there may have been more provisional miracles like this, we do know of at least two occasions where this principle worked to feed the multitudes.

Matthew 16:9-10

Do you not yet understand, neither remember the five loaves of the five thousand, and how many baskets you took up? [10]Neither the seven loaves of the four thousand, and how many baskets you took up?

The disciples knew what to expect when the demand for this miracle happened. Because they were accustomed to how this thousandfold miracle worked, they were probably not surprised that it worked every time and that there would be a surplus of prosperity from the distribution of the food.

The thousandfold blessing works through a thousandfold seed. A thousandfold seed can be something that is given in multiples of a thousand like $1,000 or it can be a gift that costs you everything.

Mark 12:41-44

And Jesus sat over against the treasury, and beheld how the people cast money into the treasury: and many that were rich cast in much. [42]And there came a certain poor widow, and she threw in two mites, which make a farthing. [43]And he called *unto him* his disciples, and said unto them, Verily I say unto you, That this poor widow hath cast more in, than all they which have cast into the treasury: [44]For all *they* did cast in of their abundance; but she of her want did cast in all that she had, *even* all her living.

This poor widow came to give that day with a purpose in mind. Her intention was to change her state of living. She threw the two small coins into the offering receptacle with expectation of a change in her financial situation. It apparently was all that she had to give because Jesus let his disciples know that she had given all she could.

It does not make sense for someone who has what was equal to two pennies to give the entire amount of money to the Lord, unless she knew what she was doing. She could have bought a morsel of bread and at least enjoyed the fruits of her two cents. The widow obviously knew what she was doing because she threw the two mites into the offering.

The word threw is the Greek word Ballo which means to throw with intense and violence. This poor widow meant business. She was absorbed with the idea of coming out of her poverty. Perhaps she had just heard the story about the widow of Sarephath and Elijah and her faith was built up to trust God with a seed in her hand.

Jesus made it a point to remark out loud about her giving on the very moment she let go of the money. He said that this poor widow gave from her state of poverty and in so doing she gave more than all the rich who gave of their abundance. In that day there was an area in the court of the Temple where the tithes and offerings were deposited. It was a container made out of metal and shaped like a funnel, kind of like toll booth coin baskets.

Jesus referenced these receptacles when He talked about the religious hypocrites that liked to sound the trumpet. We often call it tooting our own horn. Sounding the trumpet was the phrase used when someone gave a lot of money. The abundance of coins would rattle and clang as they went down into the container. The widow's mites were very small and light and they would not have made as much sound as the rich folks'

81

money did. However, Jesus could hear her intentions loud and clear.

Jesus said that her offering was larger than the entire offering of all of the rich people collectively. She did not have social security or welfare to lean on, she probably begged to get what little money she had. If her two mites offering was bigger than the total amount of money in the treasury, she deposited a thousandfold seed that was more effective than all the rich and powerful people that came to the house of God that day. Her gift did more for the Kingdom of God than the rest of the offering combined. The poor widow went from being need minded to becoming seed minded. She potentially went from a beggar to a billionaire in one day! Her seed had the power of the thousandfold blessing.

I have learned by experience that when you understand the total dynamics of the thousandfold principle, a small amount of money can go much further than its natural ability to expand. The thousandfold blessing causes the seed, large or small, to be sufficient enough for the need and more.

There are many days when all that came into my ministry was $10. Believe me, at the end of the day when we look at the bill ledger $10 does not seem sufficient. When the $10 was given from someone like the widow in Mark 12, then the thousandfold blessing causes the $10 to supernaturally meet the need of the ministry and bless the giver in thousandfold measure. Little becomes much through the thousandfold blessing.

Chapter 5
The Secret of the Thousandfold

Almost any day of the week you can tune into a Christian television network and hear preachers encourage you to sow a thousand dollars into their ministry for one reason or another. Don't misunderstand me, I believe that sowing $1,000 can be the will of God and that obeying the inspired instructions can produce incredible and miraculous results. I myself sow in multiples of thousands and encourage other people to sow in multiples of thousands.

In chapter one of this book I share some of the more notable thousandfold miracles that God has done for my family and me throughout the years. I am convinced that the thousandfold principle works because of the results that I have personally experienced. My faith in God's word and His ability is sufficient enough. I never needed any further explanation than faith produces.

However, I was always curious about why the number one thousand was such an important and powerful part of the Kingdom of God. I was convinced that there had to be a technical reason within the pages of the Bible that explain the principle in detail. In my quest for greater revelation on the subject of the thousandfold principle, I discovered that there is an absolute reason why the number one thousand is such a key number in the operation of the Kingdom of God. There is a secret about the word thousand that will open up your understanding and unlock your faith to the unlimited measure of the thousandfold in your life.

King David spoke a thousandfold blessing over the nation of Israel in the book of Psalms so that God's people would be prosperous, safe and happy. David knew that the blessing of God works through multiples of thousands. He understood that when God increases something that He does so by the thousandfold principle.

Psalm 144:13-14

That our garners *may be* full, affording all manner of store: *that* our sheep may bring forth **thousands** and ten **thousands** in our streets: [14]*That* our oxen *may be* strong to labor; *that there be* no breaking in, nor going out; that *there be* no complaining in our streets.

This is the key verse in the thousandfold principle. All of the other verses and events that took place in the Bible, and that pertain to the thousandfold principle, are built on this verse.

Of all of the verses in the word of God that contain the word thousand, this is the only verse where the word thousandfold is used. It is Strong's Hebrew #503 Alaph (a-leff) that means thousandfold. The most common word for thousand in the Old Testament Hebrew is Strong's #505 Eleph, which is defined as thousand and it is also the same word used for the Ox.

In the original Hebrew text of the original verse reads like this:

Psalm 144:13

May our storehouses constantly be filled, succeeding all types of storage places and that our sheep may bring forth **thousandfold** and ten times ten thousands in our marketplaces.

In Psalm 144 David prayed that God would cause the people to bring forth and multiply by thousandfold and ten thousands. The first word "thousands" used here in verse 13 is the only place in scripture where the word thousandfold is used.

The second word "thousands" is a different word #7231 Rabab (raw-bab) which means to multiply by a myriad. Myriad is the word for ten thousand. It comes from the root word #7241 Rabiyb (raw-beeb) which means to accumulate like rain drops. The word thousandfold is hidden because the KJV version shows it as the word thousand. But to fully interpret the scripture, the word thousandfold should be applied here.

Thousandfold is the unlimited multiplying power of God that cannot be measured by human standards. The thousandfold is God's unlimited force of multiplying power that advances the kingdom of God in every area of life. It causes the universe to constantly expand outward at light year speeds. The universe is so big because the light God spoke continues to move and expand in all directions around us. In the beginning of time, God spoke the word and the word went forth from His mouth and obediently did what He told it to do and has never stopped since.

God's plan for mankind is to be fruitful and multiply and to replenish the earth. The plan may have been hindered when sin entered the picture but God redeemed us from the curse of sin and has returned us back to the original plan.

Galatians 3:13-14
Christ has redeemed us from the curse of the law, being made a curse for us: for it is written, Cursed *is* every one that hangs on a tree: [14]That the blessing of Abraham might come on the

85

Gentiles through Jesus Christ; that we might receive the promise of the Spirit through faith.

The blessing of Abraham is a thousandfold blessing. When God told Abraham how many descendants he would have, He pointed to the elements of creation to give him a picture of the infinite volume of seed to come. The blessing of Abraham is so vast that God used the innumerable dominion of the land, the air and the sea to describe and compare with his thousandfold future.

HEAVEN
Genesis 15:5
And he brought him forth abroad, and said, Look now toward heaven, and tell the stars, if you are able to number them: and he said unto him, So shall your seed be.

EARTH
Genesis 13:16
And I will make your seed as the dust of the earth: so that if a man can number the dust of the earth, *then* shall your seed also be numbered.

SEA
Genesis 22:17
That in blessing I will bless you, and in multiplying I will multiply your seed as the stars of the heaven, and as the sand which *is* upon the sea shore; and your seed shall possess the gate of his enemies;

God showed these three elements to Abraham as a snapshot of his future. What he saw was the realm of the thousandfold. It was thousandfold because the dust, sand and stars are innumerable. God was telling Abraham that his descendants, of which you are one, would multiply in such large quantity that you would have to use these immeasurable elements for comparison.

Every time I look up to the sky at night I think of the promise that God made to his faithful friend and to the body of Christ. God has a manifold purpose in the creation of the celestials because they all glorify and speak of Him. I further believe that God placed the stars in the sky to show Abraham his future and to all of his descendants for generations to come. Symbolically you are one of those stars.

There are four words in the original Hebrew that come from the primary root word Alaph that are used for the word thousand:

- #502 Alaph: To associate with, learn, teach and utter.
- #503 Alaph: To make a thousandfold.
- #504 Eleph: A family that is yoked , like oxen, cattle.
- #505 Eleph: First letter of Hebrew alphabet , 1000, Ox.

Strong's #505 word for thousand in Hebrew is Eleph (which is pronounced eleff) and it is the first letter of the Hebrew alphabet. Eleph has a three-fold meaning.

- Thousand (associated with an unlimited measure).
- Ox (associated with the strength of 1000).
- One (first letter position in the alphabet).

All three words are synonymous with each other. The word Eleph is defined as the word ox because the original insignia for the letter, as inscribed, looks just like an ox head lowering.

See the pictorial in Figure 5-1.

The Ox head developed over time into the first
Hebrew letter Eleph, which ultimately became
the letter A.

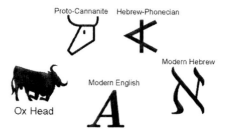

Figure 5-1

The ox is symbolic and literal in the secret of the thousandfold blessing. Symbolic because of the nature of the purpose, position and strength they represent and literal in relation to how the ox plays a very important role in the fulfillment of the thousandfold principle. The Ox possesses the strength of the number one thousand in the Kingdom of God.

There are twenty-two letters in the Hebrew language. The Hebrew text reads from right to left instead of from left to right the way that English reads. Each letter in Hebrew has a number assigned to it. For the first letter the number is 1 and then the numbers increase in groups according to the chart below.

100	ק	10	י	1	א
200	ר	20	כ,ך	2	ב
300	ש	30	ל	3	ג
400	ת	40	מ,ם	4	ד
		50	נ,ן	5	ה
		60	ס	6	ו
		70	ע	7	ז
		80	פ,ף	8	ח
		90	צ,ץ	9	ט

Figure 5-2

It is commonly believed that the Roman numeral system comes from this association of letters and numbers. There are some Jewish Rabbis who teach that there is a "secret code" within the Torah, or Book of the Law, that reveals historical facts and points to detailed prophecy. It is referred to as "The Bible Code."

Whether or not you accept the Bible code, as fact is irrelevant to my purpose in showing the Hebrew alphabet numeric value chart. The point I wish to make is that there is a wide acceptance among Jewish culture and Christians that the number and letter relation is suitable for study. This number and name association helps us better understand the truth and purpose of God's word.

In the book of 1 Kings, Solomon was anointed to be the king over the nation of Israel in the stead of his father David. Solomon realizes that his youth and inexperience do not give him the tools necessary to govern the people. He knows that this task will require wisdom beyond his years and wisdom out of this world. He determines to approach God with a specific numeric sacrifice to garner His attention so that he may personally ask God for an understanding heart to handle the job.

There is a tremendous amount of pressure put on a president or king when they enter into office. There are things that the general public does not know. There are national and international secrets that are handed over to the new leader. Now that they are in power in the office, these issues are now their responsibility to deal with. Solomon realized that he needed to tap into the power of God to obtain the wisdom of God for leadership to deal with the complexities of governing.

Solomon knew his limitations and did not over estimate his ability to reign and rule just because he wore the crown. He learned from his father and his mother how important wisdom was. He also knew that wisdom comes at a price.

Solomon gave one thousand animals in sacrifice at Gibeon to the Lord. When Solomon gave the one thousand sacrifices to God, he discovered that it would unlock the door of the secret place of the Most High God for him.

The one thousand animals were an acceptable sacrifice unto God. As a result of the thousandfold gift, God came to Solomon in a dream and met with him.

It was precisely the one thousand animals that made this event come to pass. Therefore we can conclude that there is something substantial to the number one thousand in the realm of the spirit.

The word Eleph is the first letter of the Hebrew alphabet. This gives it a first position numerically. The numeric assignment for the letter Eleph is the number 1 in the alphabetic order. When the word Eleph is applied in text it associates it with the first position of importance and it applies all of its meanings including the ox and the number one thousand to the matter.

We have established why the letter Eleph is defined as both the word thousand and the word Ox. The pictogram of the letter Eleph looks just like the head of an Ox lowering. (See Figure 5-1). A pictogram uses pictures and drawings to convey the meaning of the word or in this case the letter Eleph. So the Ox head is the symbol of the letter Eleph and therefore the word Ox, Thousand and One all have the same meaning in the Kingdom of God.

An ox was a very important part of the family farm in ancient times. Most of the sowing and harvesting was done through the power of an ox. Oxen are very large animals that are still used in many countries around the world today. They are draft animals that can plow, transport or thresh the harvest. They typically are yoked together with other oxen to increase the power and ability of the instrument it was connected to.

Oxen are multipurpose animals that do the work of the modern day tractor. The work on a farm hinges upon the condition of the tractor. When the tractor breaks, the work stops. The same thing applies to an ox. One must take care of their ox to keep the business moving. The word of God prescribes a very specific law concerning the ox.

OLD TESTAMENT

Deuteronomy 25:4
You shall not muzzle the ox when he treads out *the corn.*

NEW TESTAMENT

1 Timothy 5:17-18
Let the elders that rule well be counted worthy of double honor, especially they who labor in the word and doctrine. [18]For the scripture says, You shall not muzzle the ox that treads out the corn. And, The laborer *is* worthy of their reward.

The Law of the Ox states that it is illegal to muzzle or cover the mouth of the oxen while they are working. Paul uses this scripture to explain to the church that they should not neglect paying anointed preachers and teachers of the word. If you stop blessing the vessel of God, you stop the flow of the anointing through them. You are not only cutting off their reward, you are cutting yourself off from the revelation knowledge and truth they deliver. This is why I teach people to sow a seed with the man or woman of God whenever they receive revelation or a prophetic word from the Lord through them.

If the farmers muzzled the ox that tread out the seed, the ox would not have the strength to perform its duties. The word muzzle is the Hebrew word #2629 chacam, phonetically pronounced Khaw-sam, and it means to stop the nose. The nose draws in the breath of life; if it is blocked it cannot breath and will die. The same is true for those who function in five-fold offices. If the church does not reward them for their work, it will stop the breath of God from flowing through their words.

A messenger of God can deliver a word to an audience of people that is received by some and rejected by others. The ones that recognize the Law of the Ox will bless the messenger and be blessed in return. Those who do not will receive little or nothing from the message, even though they both hear the same word. A simpler way of saying this is, when you sow in a moment of revelation with the person delivering the message, their words will stick with you and you will have greater understanding of the message.

Recognizing the prophetic voices sent to speak into your life can be the difference between life and death. If the widow of Sarephath had not obeyed Elijah's words she and her household would have died. Her faith must have impressed God because Jesus talked about her in the New Testament. The widow in 2 Kings Chapter 4 would have lost her sons if she had not obeyed Elisha's inspired instructions to the letter.

When you recognize someone as a prophetic voice in your life you prove it with your honor towards him or her. That means you are willing to bless them financially with the understanding that God will respond to the way you treated them and He will grant you your heart's desires.

When Moses penned the Law of the Ox, God gave it to him for the people to observe and keep perpetually. It was designed to keep the oxen fed and healthy as they pulled the grinding wheel to break open the hulls of the fruit of their harvest and when they performed the other powerful tasks for the owner.

If they muzzled the oxen out while they thresh the harvest, it would prevent the oxen from eating and it would starve the animal making them grow weak and weary, rendering them useless for the purpose. This is counter-productive to the purpose of the oxen and it is counter-productive for the church. Solomon understood this law and commented on it in the book of Proverbs.

Proverbs 14:4
Where no oxen *are*, the crib *is* clean: but much increase *is* by the strength of the ox.
Living Bible
An empty stable stays clean, but there is no income from an empty stable.

When you sow a thousandfold offering before God it performs with the strength of an ox. The thousandfold seed increases the strength of the ox. So the thousandfold seed is the same as the ox that works for you to keep increase in the crib, or storage place. The stronger the ox, the greater the harvest will be.

On the farm the Israelites generally had at least one ox that they depended on for food and income. Some farms had teams of oxen with over twenty yoke of oxen. This would be similar to the huge combines used on corporate farms in America. Those machines require a lot of fuel to operate. If you do not put gasoline or diesel fuel in the tank, they simply will not run and you will not get any benefit from them.

The same thing is true in the church today. You cannot expect the man or woman of God to perform well if they are not properly compensated. This is a spiritual law that is supported by the law of the ox. A local church should be very concerned with the compensation of their teachers within the five-fold ministry. I believe that if you do not care about the pay for the pastor or prophet of God, that you will advance no further than the compensation you reward them with. Your revelation is directly connected to their compensation.

In many cases, the church board has attempted to control the five-fold ministry, especially the pastor. This quenches the flow of the revelation of the word of God and the power and anointing that follows. You cannot legislate, regulate or interrogate the power of God. When a church board comprised of deacons and elders tries to manipulate and control the pastor, it muzzles the breath of God from the people.

God delivers the message to the pastor and the pastor delivers it to the people. The pastor, like all other five-fold offices, is a gift from God to the people. The old saying, "Don't look a gift horse in the mouth" could be said in this case, "Don't muzzle a gifted Pastor's mouth."

The world portrays "Men of the Cloth" as weak, powerless and impoverished people. The idea that men of God should take a vow of poverty is a man-made idea but has absolutely no scriptural support. It is a demonic doctrine designed to undermine the communication between believers and the five-fold ministers.

We are to honor the anointed men and women of God that work hard to deliver the word of God to us, both through instruction and impartation. In fact, they are worthy of "double honor" or twice the pay for their efforts. If the church continues to refuse supporting and sowing into anointed vessels, then it will stifle the revelation of the word of God and will eventually discourage the preachers and teachers of the word.

This happened during the reign of Ahaz the king. Because the Temple was neglected and the people stopped giving, the Levite Priests became discouraged and left to take other jobs. Ahaz's son Hezekiah restored the Temple and commanded the return of the tithes to the Lord. This encouraged the return of the Levite Priests. Without the Priesthood there was no service in the house of God. The offerings and the restoration of the Priesthood brought the glory of God back to the house.

The idea of connecting a $1,000 seed to the glory of God is unthinkable in religious circles. They reject the idea of God moving as a result of a seed sown. You will have to shake off religious ideas and opinions in order to flow in the thousandfold blessing and lifestyle.

My wife and I have a personal commitment to bless the anointed vessels that speak into our lives. When we give by thousandfold we are tapping into the instruction and impartation, the knowledge and the revelation of that vessel. If I disobeyed the instruction of the Holy Spirit, I for all intents and purposes shut the mouth of the prophet of God speaking into my life. I don't always give at thousand dollar levels but if I am compelled by the Holy Spirit to do it, and it is in my power to give it, I am inclined to obey.

Many people attend a meeting, watch a broadcast or read the book of someone who can transfer the tangible anointing upon their life, but they fail to get it because they don't see the connection between the man of God and the power of God. They hear the instruction but they do not get the impartation. You can listen to someone talk about driving a car but until you have the keys in your hand and a vehicle to match, you will not know what it is like for yourself. Even if you get into the car it will do nothing unless there is gas in the tank. Blessing the Ox financially insures that the power and anointing of God upon them blesses you and your household.

The prophet Ezekiel said that the first fruit offerings of the people were to be given to the Priest and that the Priest would cause the blessing to rest upon the houses of the people.

Ezekiel 44:30
And the first of all the firstfruits of all *things*, and every oblation of all, of every *sort* of your oblations, shall be the priest's: you shall also give unto the priest the first of your dough, that he may cause the blessing to rest in your house.

This verse is not speaking of giving the offerings to the church; it is expressly speaking of giving the gift to the individual man or woman of God. In the thousandfold principle, your man or woman of God is the Ox that helps plow for your life.

There is another Oxen Law that had to be observed by the people of God. You could not yoke an ox with a donkey.

96

Deuteronomy 22:10
You shall not plow with an ox and a donkey together.

Plowing with an ox and a donkey would be unequally yoked. The two animals are different in weight, size, temperament and purpose. The ox is five to six times heavier than the donkey. More importantly, the ox is tame and the donkey is wild. The team would be double minded and they would not accomplish the same task for their master. This is like the double-minded person that cannot receive anything from the Lord.

When you decide to act upon the thousandfold principle there will be people who misunderstand, and perhaps that will oppose you and try to pull you away from it. Let me encourage you to stay on course and remain yoked with Jesus.

In the Bible most families had one or maybe two oxen to yoke together and plow. If you had more than two you were considered a wealthy person indeed. In 1 Kings Chapter 19, Elisha was plowing with twelve yoke of oxen when Elijah placed his mantle of anointing upon his neck.

1 Kings 19:19-21
So he departed thence, and found Elisha the son of Shaphat, who *was* plowing *with* twelve yoke *of oxen* before him, and he with the twelfth: and Elijah passed by him, and cast his mantle upon him. [20]And he left the oxen, and ran after Elijah, and said, Let me, I pray you, kiss my father and my mother, and *then* I will follow you. And he said unto him, Go back again: for what have I done to you? [21]And he returned back from him, and took a yoke of oxen, and slew them, and boiled their flesh with the instruments of the oxen, and gave unto the people, and they

did eat. Then he arose, and went after Elijah, and ministered unto him.

Twelve yoke of oxen equates to twelve pairs for a total of 24 oxen. Elisha must have been a skilled driver with command over a team this large. Elisha's family must have owned a rather large parcel of land to need that many oxen to plow the field. How powerful a team these animals must have been. Elisha chose to sacrifice two of these animals to honor the prophet of God and then he burnt the plow. Burning the plow has to do with moving forward. As long as there is a plow to return to, it can be very easy to give up and go back home. If the plow is destroyed there are no other options than to proceed.

Elisha understood that there would be a price to pay for the power of God. He walked away from everything he had to serve Elijah. Another way of saying he attended to his needs while Elijah ministered. The result for Elisha was a double portion of the same anointing that was upon Elijah. The price to obtain it included the oxen. The ox represents the thousandfold offering. Elisha gave two oxen as a sacrifice to feed Elijah and all the people. The two oxen foreshadow the double portion anointing that would come upon Elisha after Elijah left the earth.

Like Solomon, Elisha wanted something specific and he was willing to do what it took to get there. Elisha operated in the thousandfold principle when he sacrificed the oxen and burnt the plow behind him. When you decide to give everything that you have for the Gospel, the thousandfold principle takes effect. Elisha recognized and honored the prophet Elijah with his thousandfold offering which in turn energized the thousandfold blessing in his life.

Honor is part of the reward of the thousandfold. In addition to wisdom from God, Solomon received honor, riches and long life. Honor is high regard and esteem for someone's ability, achievements and character coupled with admiration, or even adoration, for the person. A simple way to say this is:

Respect + Love = Honor

A thousandfold believer is a person of honor. Honoring an anointed man or woman of God is vital to your success. Dishonoring God's anointed prophets intentionally or ignorantly can bring devastating consequences.

The secret of the word thousand and its meaning in the Kingdom of God is not as hard to find as some may think. The secret to the word thousand is found in the connection between the oxen which represents the significant prophetic voice you listen to and the number 1000. The thousandfold principle is in force whenever you give to God in multiples of thousands, or with a gift, which represents your thousandfold faith.

God chose 1000 as the number that unlocks the unlimited power of God and opens up the Secret Place of the Most High God. However, it is apparent that the thousand is used over and over again in the Bible as the catalyst for miracles, signs and wonders. Like anything you hear about, you must take time to investigate its validity. I have spent the better part of twenty-five years in search of the full meaning and purpose and I continue to seek God for greater wisdom on the thousandfold.

I believe that thousand is the base number in the Kingdom of God and in all of creation. You must decide for yourself. As for me, the faith God gave to me, and the notable miracles that

God has performed in my life are evidence enough to support the thousandfold principle. I believe that God will release the same powerful force of the thousandfold principle in your life when you wrap your faith around the word and launch out into the deep!

Chapter 6

Thousandfold Seed

Everyone dreams when they sleep. Dreams are the subject of clinical studies, countless books, movies and discussions. According to Oneirology, which is the scientific study of dreams, the average person dreams a total of six years during their lifetime. That amounts to about two hours a night. Most dreams are five to twenty minutes in length and contrary to common belief, most dreams are in color not in black and white

There are varied opinions as to the origin and interpretation of dreams. They range from subconscious reflection to divine communication. God speaks to people in dreams or night visions to establish His purpose in your life. He accesses your spirit when you are at rest. Job's friend Elihu said that God does this when you fall into a deep sleep.

Job 33:14-18
For God speaks once, yes twice, *yet man* perceives it not. [15]In a dream, in a vision of the night, when deep sleep falls upon men, in slumberings upon the bed; [16]Then he opens the ears of men, and seals their instruction, [17]That he may withdraw man *from his* purpose, and hide pride from man. [18]He keeps back his soul from the pit, and his life from perishing by the sword.

Dreams are one of the ways that God communicates with His people. From Genesis to Revelation there are many instances where God speaks to, warns and interacts with people. Here are some examples of dreams in the Bible:

101

- Abimelech was warned in a dream by God not to touch Sarah.
- Abraham dreamed about Israel's deliverance from Egypt.
- Jacob saw God in a dream and vowed to be a tither.
- Joseph dreamed about saving his family and the world.
- Daniel dreamed about the kingdoms of the future.
- Joseph was warned by God to protect Jesus and Mary.
- John dreamed about end time events.

Dreams and visions are a part of the fulfillment of the promise of the outpouring of the Holy Spirit on the Day of Pentecost. Dreams and visions allow us to interface with God outside the natural realm, which tends to limit our thinking and hinder our progress. They are embedded in our spirit and become a part of us. They allow us to experience the future and they give something to hold onto and to hope for.

My entire ministry was revealed to me in a dream. When I was sixteen years old, I had a dream that God took me into heaven and showed me my future. In the dream I met the Lord Jesus Christ. I met with Him face to face like a friend would. He was wearing casual attire and He was about six feet tall. I don't remember the details of His face, hair or eye color but I recall what He showed me and how He communicated with me.

During the course of the dream Jesus showed me control rooms full of television equipment. The technology that I saw was way ahead of its time. The Lord showed me a sign with words that said I would one day be the president of a group of Christian TV stations. However, I was not interested in television, I was interested in radio. My life's goal before the dream was to be a disc jockey on a big radio station in New York City.

Afterwards the Lord stood facing me about three feet away. I had lots of questions about the things that He had shown me and as these questions went through my mind I wanted to open my mouth and speak, but instead a slow steady stream of light proceeded from my belly moving towards Jesus. I call it a stream because it was translucent and seemed to have elements moving around in the light.

Before the light stream entered into the belly of the Lord a stream of light came forth from His belly and entered into mine. I instantly knew that He was answering all of my questions and that He was depositing the information and ability in me to fulfill the dream. Neither one of us ever opened our mouth to communicate. We were communicating from spirit to spirit.

I wrote the dream down and handed it to my mother who kept the piece of paper and gave it back to me when, at the age of twenty-five I launched out in ministry. For over twenty-five years I have been the president of a group of Christian TV stations in America. This dream is still alive and reaching thousands for the Lord every day.

Earlier we looked at the first mention of the application of the thousandfold principle concerning Abimelech and Sarah. God spoke to Abimelech in a dream to warn him not to touch Sarah. Abimelech gave Sarah's husband Abraham one thousand pieces of silver to redeem him from destruction and to vindicate Sarah. There was a definite connection between the one thousand pieces of silver given to Abraham and the dream Abimelech had from God.

King Solomon sacrificed one thousand animals to God on an altar at Gibeon with the purpose of obtaining an understanding

103

heart to rule the nation of Israel. His gift was a thousandfold seed.

1 Kings 3:1-4

And Solomon made affinity with Pharaoh king of Egypt, and took Pharaoh's daughter, and brought her into the city of David, until he had made an end of building his own house, and the house of the LORD, and the wall of Jerusalem round about. ²Only the people sacrificed in high places, because there was no house built unto the name of the LORD, until those days. ³And Solomon loved the LORD, walking in the statutes of David his father: only he sacrificed and burnt incense in high places. ⁴And the king went to Gibeon to sacrifice there; for that *was* the great high place: a thousand burnt offerings did Solomon offer upon that altar.

Solomon was the son of King David and his wife Bathsheba. David chose to place Solomon on the throne of Israel in his stead. Solomon's primary purpose was to oversee the construction of the Temple of God that David desired to build. David gathered most of the materials from the spoils of war for the construction of the Temple. Some of the resources came through trade and negotiations between Solomon and his father's allies. King David admonished Solomon to pursue wisdom and to serve God with a perfect heart.

1 Chronicles 28:9-10

And you, Solomon my son, know you the God of your father, and serve him with a perfect heart and with a willing mind: for the LORD searches all hearts, and understands all the imaginations of the thoughts: if you seek him, he will be found of you; but if you forsake him, he will cast you off for ever.

¹⁰Take heed now; for the LORD has chosen you to build a house for the sanctuary: be strong, and do *it*.

David then prayed to God that He would give Solomon a perfect heart to fulfill the duties of the throne of Israel and to build the palace of God.

1 Chronicles 29:19
And give unto Solomon my son a perfect heart, to keep Your commandments, Your testimonies, and Your statutes, and to do all *these things*, and to build the palace, *for* which I have made provision.

Solomon was a young man when he was anointed to be the king of Israel and he knew that he would need more than a crown to finish this seven-year project. The building was to be hand-made to the specifications of king David. David wanted to build the Temple, but David could not until he made all of his enemies his footstool around him. David defeated all of the enemies of Israel and then there was peace and rest on every side around Solomon who would take the project on.

The workmen were people of wisdom that custom crafted the stones and materials that the building was comprised of. The Temple was built without noise and confusion to represent the peace of God. Solomon's name means peace and during the forty years he reigned on the throne, peace was all he ever knew because David had defeated all the enemies around them. David must have done a thorough job to keep the enemies back for such a long period of time.

Solomon was a young man that did not have any previous experience of any kind, let alone leading a nation. He knew that he was going to need a crash course in wisdom in order to handle the assignment that was now upon him. In his quest for understanding, he made a decision to present a sacrifice to God on top of the hill of Gibeon. His purpose was to get God's attention so that he could ask for wisdom and understanding to equip him for the task.

Solomon sought God for wisdom and understanding to deal wisely with the matters of the nation and to build the house of God. He knew that in order to complete this project it would require favor and skills to negotiate for the materials and skilled labor to build the dwelling place that would bring the glory of God and the name of God to the Temple.

1 Kings 3:5-9

In Gibeon the LORD appeared to Solomon in a dream by night: and God said, Ask what I shall give you. [6]And Solomon said, You have showed unto your servant David my father great mercy, according as he walked before you in truth, and in righteousness, and in uprightness of heart with you; and you have kept for him this great kindness, that you have given him a son to sit on his throne, as *it is* this day. [7]And now, O LORD my God, you have made your servant king instead of David my father: and I *am but* a little child: I know not *how* to go out or come in. [8]And your servant *is* in the midst of your people which you have chosen, a great people, that cannot be numbered nor counted for multitude. [9]Give therefore your servant an understanding heart to judge your people, that I may discern between good and bad: for who is able to judge this your so great a people?

This is a defining moment in his life that was also very important to the future of the nation of Israel. God told

Solomon that he could ask anything he wanted and He would give it to him. Solomon could have asked for all the fame, fortune and happiness in the world but he did not. Solomon narrowed his request down to wisdom, which is the most important thing in the world.

1 Kings 3:10-14
And the speech pleased the LORD, that Solomon had asked this thing. [11]And God said unto him, Because you have asked this thing, and have not asked for yourself long life; neither have asked riches for yourself, nor have asked the life of your enemies; but have asked for yourself understanding to discern judgment; [12]Behold, I have done according to your words: lo, I have given you a wise and an understanding heart; so that there was none like you before you, neither after you shall any arise like unto you. [13]And I have also given you that which you have not asked, both riches, and honor: so that there shall not be any among the kings like unto you all your days. [14]And if you will walk in my ways, to keep my statutes and my commandments, as your father David did walk and then I will lengthen your days.

When you sow a thousandfold seed it opens up the right of entry to ask God for an unlimited request. The thousandfold is an unlimited measure. The thousandfold seed activates the open-ended petition process. Solomon could have asked for absolutely anything that he wanted. God would have given him the moon if he so desired. If Solomon had asked for the moon, his request would have been met in full measure or the hundredfold. God is able to do above all that we ask or think, so when Solomon requested an understanding heart filled with Godly wisdom, it opened the floodgate for God to release all of the unlimited things that wisdom produces.

When Solomon presented the thousandfold sacrifice to God he did it on top of the hill of Gibeon. It is important to note that Gibeon was set on a high hill. It was the tradition of the day to sacrifice to the different gods on tops of hills and mountains. The god that was celebrated on the highest mountain would be known as the preeminent, or highest of the gods. We know that there is only one true God, Jehovah. He is also known as El-Elyon, the Most High God, the possessor of Heaven and earth and the deliverer of all your enemies including lack, debt, poverty, and scarceness.

Solomon had to exert a great effort to bring one thousand gifts to God when he climbed up the hill of Gibeon with each and every one of the animals. That's a lot of work no matter how you approach it. If what you give to God does not expend you and elevate your position, then you have not tapped into the thousandfold principle. King David said, "I will not offer that which cost me nothing." David made this statement when he purchased the ground that the Temple was built upon. Solomon was aware of this and he knew that the wisdom he pursued would cost him something as well.

Solomon must have been exhausted after completing this mission. I suppose we would all be fast asleep after bringing a thousand animals up a hill and slaying them before God. It is not always easy to give at times.

When my wife and I began to bring the tithes and offerings to the Lord, it was not convenient. We were a young couple raising a family on a tight budget while building a small business and working in the ministry. We learned to trust God with all of our heart and all of our money. The tithe was always ten percent of our gross income and our offerings varied in size.

Every week we would challenge each other to increase our offering amount above the tithe. We generally bumped it up between five or ten dollars a week.

We tithed because we feared the Lord always but we gave offerings because we loved Him. We disciplined our finances and made sure that we never robbed God. It was difficult at times, but we never let the situations around us get the upper hand. As God prospered us we were able to give larger amounts of money in the offerings and we eventually reached a point when we could give a $1,000 or more. The day we were able to give a $1,000 was a defining moment for us.

Solomon's request was not a selfish one. His appeal to God was for something that affected the lives of the entire population of the nation of Israel. Solomon did not ask for things, he asked for a perfect heart to understand and to reign as king. Solomon asked for wisdom and God gave him according to what he said. In addition, God gave Solomon wisdom, riches and peace. Wisdom is what produces money, honor and life. If you are facing a money problem, getting more money is not the answer, more wisdom is what you need. Solomon sought the Lord with a thousandfold seed in his hands. God then made the things that Solomon needed to build the Temple to look for him. Jesus said:

Matthew 6:33
But seek you first the kingdom of God, and his righteousness; and all these things shall be added unto you.

All the things that Solomon needed to build the House of the Lord came towards him. When you seek for wisdom you will not have to seek for things because things will look for you.

The thousandfold seed produced a thousandfold blessing for Solomon that created incredible wealth for the building of his own houses. Solomon had a house that took thirteen years to build, and in addition to that he had a house in the forest of Lebanon, kind of like a summer home, and he built a house for his wives.

The things that were added to Solomon's life came to him as a bonus from God as a result of his thousandfold seed. God is able to go far beyond whatever we ask or think of but it is conditioned on the activation of the power that works in us.

Ephesians 3:20-21
Now unto him that is able to do exceeding abundantly above all that we ask or think, according to the power that works in us, [21]Unto him *be* glory in the church by Christ Jesus throughout all ages, world without end. Amen.

God blessed Solomon beyond his wildest dreams. God wants to do the same thing for you. When Solomon awoke from his dream, the favor and blessing of God caused immense amounts of wealth and riches to magnetically attract towards him.

In the dream God appeared to Solomon and gave him a "blank check" to ask Him for anything that he wanted. This was a direct result of the thousandfold seed that Solomon offered. Obviously God is moved by this offering and is drawn towards Solomon. The thousandfold gift opened up a door for Solomon that revealed God's person and His presence to him.

There are only a few occasions in the Bible where people had a personal encounter with God. Adam walked with Him in the Garden of Eden, Abraham saw God in a vision in Genesis Chapter 15, Jacob saw God in a dream in Genesis Chapter 28, Moses saw Him in a cloud face-to-face and Solomon sees God in this dream.

The key to this encounter is connected to the thousandfold seed. One thousand is a large number of anything, no matter what you are counting. There is something about the number 1000 that moves you. Thousand is a qualifier in the Kingdom of God. Solomon's one thousand sacrifices qualified him to have an appointment with God. Solomon did not give $1,000 dollars, he gave one thousand animals worth more that $1,000. The thousandfold seed is qualified by one of two things:

- The gift is exactly 1,000 units.
- The gift costs you everything.

If you give $1,000 dollars for something, you have presented one thousand one-dollar bills. If you give $100 dollars you have given a thousand dimes to the Lord. If you give $10 you have presented a thousand pennies to the Lord. Each denomination of money can be divided into multiples of a thousand. This is vital information for every believer to know, because the thousandfold principle applies to the units given whether it is a thousand dollars or a thousand rubies.

Solomon did not give $1,000 he gave 1,000 units. He was in a position to give at this level because of the family fortune that his father David had amassed from the spoils of war. The thousandfold seed that Solomon gave to God was worth far more than $1,000. Each of the animals was worth more than a thousand of any currency.

111

The reason I break this down this way is so that you can see that anyone can tap into the thousandfold blessing no matter what their financial condition or status is. Let me make this point perfectly clear. The one thousand units of money must represent your ability to give. If you can write a check for ten dollars and never miss it, you have not tapped into the thousandfold principle. If what you gave cost you something, then it will move you and it will move God towards you.

The purpose of an altar is to present a sacrifice that invites God's presence. God is never obligated to come to an empty altar. The cross was the altar that God used to give His son Jesus to the whole world for the redemption of sin. The cross without the Savior would be just another tree.

The thousandfold principle is not just connected to a $1,000 seed alone. The thousandfold principle is connected to a thousand units or individual items given at a time. When Solomon became the king of Israel he gave a thousand burnt offerings to the Lord. Remember, thousand is a multiplier. So in this case, the thousand was multiplied times the market value of the animals presented to the Lord. The average ox weighs 2,500 pounds. That is nearly the size of a compact car.

If you look at the livestock market price for a steer, they are going for about $90.00 per hundred pound. If an average steer weighs 1,000 pounds, then the market price per head would be $900. If an ox weighs 2,500 pounds and you used the $90.00 per hundred pound formula, you would arrive at $2,250.00 per ox. If you multiply 1000 animals times $2,250.00 per animal, that would equal to $2,250,000.00 (two million, two hundred fifty thousand dollars). Where I live, the state fair will hold a competition for prized animals. Some of the award-winning steers are worth over $250,000.00 a piece. This is based on the value of its quality and characteristics, not just the per pound value.

Consider how much time and effort was invested in birthing and raising the animals that were given to God. The collective costs of taking care of a herd of 1000 bulls or heifers is staggering. There is food, water, shelter, labor, medical attention, and transportation expenses, just to name a few.

I outlined this for your benefit, so that you may get a better picture of the full monetary value of the offering that Solomon gave to the Lord in Gibeon. In the example above, the one thousand animals were worth more than $1,000 dollars each. Beyond this fact, the greater value of the animal is measured by its life. What price can you place on a life? God placed the price of the blood of Jesus on you because He sees you as a prized possession, and because He loves you and was willing to do whatever it took to prove that love to you and save you.

Solomon's father David believed in giving your best offering to God and he raised Solomon the same way. Solomon learned to trust that God would bless and multiply the gifts that he gave. He further understood that the thousandfold principle was initiated by giving in thousandfold measure and that it would invoke the Lord's presence. Solomon began his search for wisdom by sowing a thousand units at a time and he continued to give by the same measure throughout his life.

1 Kings 8:63

And Solomon offered a sacrifice of peace offerings, which he offered unto the LORD, two and twenty thousand oxen, and an hundred and twenty thousand sheep. So the king and all the children of Israel dedicated the house of the LORD.

113

When the House of God was completed, Solomon determined to continue giving to God by the thousands. This time he offered 22 times the number of animals that he did at Gibeon, and he has given an additional 120,000 sheep to boot. Solomon believed in giving to God in thousandfold multiples. It took seven years to complete the Temple and during the course of those seven years God has multiplied Solomon's livestock by the myriads. God has multiplied his offering 22 times over 7 years. If the thousandfold seed worked to give Solomon his petition of God, then the thouandfold seed would continue to work in other offerings. Once you move into the realm of the thousandfold why change?

The purpose of the original thousandfold was to open the door of wisdom in his life so that he could judge the nation fairly. The blessing of God added to his request and brought him untold riches, long life, safety and the thousandfold anointing of God. The anointing of God multiplied his offering by the thousandfold measure. Solomon's offering had grown so large that the area where the brass or burnt altar was positioned was too small to receive the sacrifice, so Solomon enlarged the area where the animals could be slain.

1 Kings 8:64-65

The same day did the king hallow the middle of the court that *was* before the house of the LORD: for there he offered burnt offerings, and meat offerings, and the fat of the peace offerings: because the brasen altar that *was* before the LORD *was* too little to receive the burnt offerings, and meat offerings, and the fat of the peace offerings. [65]And at that time Solomon held a feast, and all Israel with him, a great congregation, from the entering in of Hamath unto the river of Egypt, before the LORD our God, seven days and seven days, *even* fourteen days.

The original thousandfold offering Solomon brought to God at Gibeon was completed in one day and then that night God came to him in a dream. The offering of the dedication of the Temple took fourteen days to complete. Imagine walking in the thousandfold blessing that would position you to bring a continual offering to God for two straight weeks. If the original thousandfold seed produced billions of dollars in wealth, what would the Temple dedication offering produce?

When Solomon dedicated the Temple he had to enlarge the offering area because there was not enough room to receive the sacrifices on the altar. God had increased Solomon's ability to sow by thousands more than he originally did at Gibeon. The ground upon which the offering was given was called "Holy Ground." In order for the offering to be acceptable it had to be presented on Holy Ground. When Solomon's offering increased, the area of the ground had to be expanded to receive the offering.

The size of Solomon's offering demanded a larger area, which expanded the area of holiness. I believe that when we increase our giving to the Lord, that the territory of our holiness enlarges as well. Holy ground is the place where the miraculous power of God flows. It is the place where you meet with God and He gives you instruction and purpose and it is the platform for the meeting in the Secret Place of the Most High God.

Solomon's offering was bigger than the altar. The solution to the problem was to increase the area for the offering between the altar and the porch of the Temple and declare it to be Holy Ground. Solomon increased the boundaries of the Holy Ground by enlarging his offering in increments of thousands.

Solomon went from offering 1,000 animals to God at Gibeon, to offering 142,000 animals in sacrifice to the Lord at the Temple.

Every Christian should desire to give to God according to the Biblical instruction pertaining to tithes, offerings, first fruits and alms giving. They should also desire to increase the measure of their giving until they tap into the thousandfold level. The Bible says that we go from faith to faith and from glory to glory. You should advance from giving to giving as well.

I learned by experience through the years that when I sowed a thousandfold seed, it did something to increase my faith and understanding in the word of God. It taught me how to trust in the Lord with all of my heart and with all of my finances. Something unexplainable always happens inside me when I give with thousandfold faith. God deposits a supernatural peace and serenity that lets me know that He accepts my thousandfold seed and He is at work on my behalf.

I believe that the measure you give by will be the measure that you live by. Living by the thousandfold is a lifestyle, not an event. God's Kingdom operates and flows through the thousandfold principle. The kingdom of God is built on and established by the principle of seed power. Jesus said that the Kingdom of God is the same as if a person were to cast seed into the ground.

Every battle in life is fought and won through a seed sown. God won the battle for the souls of mankind by sowing Jesus as the ultimate thousandfold seed. The principles of the kingdom of God are eternal and will be the principles by which the kingdom of God is governed forever. The thousandfold seed and all of the things that it produces will continue for all eternity. The way that you develop in this world will determine the position you will work from for the rest of your life.

Those who choose to function through the thousandfold principle now will be trusted to reign and rule with all of the thousandfold benefits of the kingdom of God without end.

Chapter 7
Thousandfold Wisdom

Wisdom is the principal thing in life. Everything that God does comes from the wisdom of His word. Reading the Bible is not enough to explain the meaning of the scriptures, you must have revelation that enlightens the word for you.

Wisdom is obtained through:

- Study of the word.
- Prayer and supplication.
- Sowing a seed.

God gives us keys to unlock the mysteries of His Kingdom and the faith to believe and conceive them. These keys are hidden in the wisdom of the scriptures. God is very good at hiding things, but He gives you wisdom to open up the mysteries of the Kingdom. Searching the scriptures will reveal the truths of God 's word that will reward and promote your life. You must diligently pursue wisdom to discover it.

Proverbs 25:2
It is the glory of God to conceal a thing: but the honor of kings *is* to search out a matter.

Conceal in the Hebrew means to cover. God's glory covers his word. Everything that God created must have a covering. Sin and the curse removed the covering of the Lord from man, but Jesus returned it back to us on the Day of Penetecost. Honor is the same word as glory.

The glory of kings comes from the Glory of God. The book of Revelation says that believers are kings and priests that reign and rule with Him. When a believer searches the word, it produces the glory of God in your life and then the word of God is revealed to you. Jesus said to search the scriptures for in them you will find life. The scriptures contain the ageless wisdom of God to live your life by.

The word search means to penetrate and examine, like a surgeon who performs exploratory surgery. Until they cut through the flesh they cannot observe the internal organs of the body. When you diligently examine the scriptures, you will break through the layer of your flesh that prevents you from seeing the deeper meaning of the word of God and it will unlock the wisdom of God for you. The wisdom of God is the way that God thinks, speaks and does things.

Wisdom is the master key that unlocks the operation of the principles and truths of the entire thousandfold Kingdom. Wisdom does not come to you, wisdom is found by searching for it.

Proverbs 4:5-7
Get wisdom, get understanding: forget *it* not; neither decline from the words of my mouth. [6]Forsake her not, and she shall preserve you: love her, and she shall keep you. [7]Wisdom *is* the principal thing; *therefore* get wisdom: and with all your getting get understanding.

Wisdom comes at a price. The question you must ask yourself is, "What is the price that I am willing to pay for it?" Like anything in life, the more you pay for something the greater the value. Some people are willing to pursue just enough wisdom to make them feel comfortable while others are willing to go further. Job made a comparison of wisdom.

Job 28:18b

...for the price of wisdom *is* above rubies.

Job says that the price of wisdom is far above the price of rubies. Rubies are generally not the most expensive gems on the market. There are many other precious gems that are priced much higher than rubies, even though there are fewer rubies than any other gem in the world. The reason that Job said this is because in actuality there are far fewer rubies in the earth than there are diamonds and sapphires.

Rubies are distinguished and known for their fiery red color. It is a most desirable gem due to its hardness, durability, luster, and rarity. Transparent rubies of large sizes are even more rare than diamonds. Transparent, flawless rubies can exceed all other gems in value. Rubies must be transparent to possess high gem value.

Wisdom is compared to the price of rubies because they are rare and beautiful. Rubies are also known to be the hardest among precious gems. Their ardent texture allows it to endure for extremely long periods of time. Wisdom will give you the durability to make it in the long haul.

In the Old Testament, God instructed Moses to make the clothes and ornaments for the High Priest for beauty and for glory unto God. He gave Moses very specific detail of the robes and of the things that would be attached to the garments of the High Priest. One of the items the High Priest wore was the breastplate. The breastplate was adorned with twelve different stones representing the twelve tribes of Israel.

121

Exodus 39:8-15

And he made the breastplate *of* cunning work, like the work of the ephod; *of* gold, blue, and purple, and scarlet, and fine twined linen. ⁹It was foursquare; they made the breastplate double: a span *was* the length thereof, and a span the breadth thereof, *being* doubled. ¹⁰And they set in it four rows of stones: *the first* row *was* a sardius, a topaz, and a carbuncle: this *was* the first row. ¹¹And the second row, an emerald, a sapphire, and a diamond. ¹²And the third row, a ligure, an agate, and an amethyst. ¹³And the fourth row, a beryl, an onyx, and a jasper: *they were* inclosed in ouches of gold in their inclosings. ¹⁴And the stones *were* according to the names of the children of Israel, twelve, according to their names, *like* the engravings of a signet, every one with his name, according to the twelve tribes. ¹⁵And they made upon the breastplate chains at the ends, *of* wreathen work *of* pure gold.

The first stone mounted on the breastplate is called a sardius. Sardius is another name for the word ruby. It comes from the Hebrew word O-dem, which means ruby or redness. The root word for O-dem is aw-dam, which means to show blood. It is also the name of the first man God created, Adam. So we see here that God made Adam with the nature of wisdom.

Each of the twelve stones on the breastplate had an engraving on them. The engraving, or signet, was inscribed in the precious gems to identify the name of the particular tribe with the stone. When we use nametags to identify people we often use a cheap paper label stuck to the lapel of one's garment. God uses precious gems as nametags for His people. God values His people above silver, gold and precious stones.

The question of whose names are on which stones has been the subject of much debate. The Bible does not detail which stones had which names assigned to them in this chapter of Exodus, but it is commonly understood that the order they are written in is the order they were laid out in. The ruby represents the tribe of Judah. Judah was always first in line in the ranks of the tribes and Judah was always the first tribe to be sent in marching order. Judah is the tribe of the kings of Israel and the tribe Jesus came from. The ruby also represents the blood of Jesus that was shed at Calvary for the sins of the whole world.

The price of wisdom is far above rubies. So there is a price for wisdom and the closest we can account to it is the price of a ruby. Given that the ruby is first in order on the breastplate and wisdom is the first, or principal thing, in life it serves to prove that wisdom comes at a great price. The New Testament book of James states that wisdom is a matter of asking God.

James 1:5
If any of you lack wisdom, let them ask of God, that gives to all liberally, and upbraids not; and it shall be given them.

James did not say that wisdom was free, he said that God is the one who gives wisdom to those who ask for it. There is a price for anything of value. If you pay nothing for something that is what you will think it is worth. The emphasis on James 1:5 is not on the word "ask" but rather on the word "all." James made this statement to establish that God is not a respecter of person. In other words everyone is eligible to obtain the wisdom of God who asks for it, but there will be a cost associated with the request.

123

Salvation is a free gift from God. You do not have to work for it. You receive your salvation by grace through faith in Jesus Christ. As a Christian you are given faith as a measure from God to believe in Him. The faith that God gives to you will enable you to receive and activate the promises of God's word for you. The hearing of the word of God is what causes you to increase in faith. The more you hear the word of God the greater your faith expands, like a muscle that is exercised. The anointing of God is what empowers and manifests the ability of God's word. The definition of the anointing of God is the ability of God to do great and mighty exploits.

The price to obtain wisdom includes: time, diligence, humility, and money. Whether you attend a university for higher learning or become a student of a mentor, the bottom line is that there will be a price for your education. The price of wisdom becomes more efficient when you are connected to someone who has expertise in his or her field of knowledge. That is why having a mentor in your life is so important.

When you find the wisdom you are looking for you should want to know more. When you have made a qualified decision to obtain wisdom you should be willing to do whatever it takes to have it, just like the men in the parable of the pearl of great price.

Matthew 13:44-46

Again, the kingdom of heaven is like unto treasure hid in a field; the which when a man has found, he hides, and for joy thereof goes and sells all that he has, and buys that field. [45]Again, the kingdom of heaven is like unto a merchant man, seeking goodly pearls: [46]Who, when he had found one pearl of great price, went and sold all that he had, and bought it.

The price you are willing to pay will determine the pearl that you will possess. The pearl in the parable is wisdom. Once you possess the pearl of wisdom you are looking for you should spare no expense in protecting it.

In 1 Kings Chapter 3, King Solomon determined to get the wisdom he needed to rule the kingdom of Israel. Solomon pursued God's wisdom with a thousandfold seed in his hands. Solomon would become the richest and wisest king of his time. Solomon was used by God to write 3,000 proverbs and 1,005 songs. Solomon was anointed with a thousandfold anointing. The thousandfold anointing causes everything you touch to reproduce in multiples of thousands.

If Solomon had not sown the thousandfold animal sacrifice unto God at Gibeon, we may not have had the thousandfold pearls that the wisdom books of Proverbs, Ecclesiastes and Song of Solomon offers. Solomon's thousandfold seed became God's opportunity to give the human race the insight and revelation of wisdom of eternity.

The thousandfold seed that Solomon gave to God at Gibeon came back to him in multiples of thousands. From the time that God met with Solomon in the dream, Solomon began to flow in God's thousandfold wisdom.

1 Kings 4:29-34
And God gave Solomon wisdom and understanding exceeding much, and largeness of heart, even as the sand that *is* on the seashore. [30]And Solomon's wisdom excelled the wisdom of all the children of the east country, and all the wisdom of Egypt. [31]For he was wiser than all men; than Ethan the Ezrahite, and Heman, and Chalcol, and Darda, the sons of Mahol: and his fame was in all nations round about. [32]And he spake three

thousand proverbs: and his songs were a thousand and five. [33]And he spoke of trees, from the cedar tree that *is* in Lebanon even unto the hyssop that springs out of the wall: he spoke also of beasts, and of fowl, and of creeping things, and of fishes. [34]And there came of all people to hear the Wisdom of Solomon, from all kings of the earth, which had heard of his wisdom.

The thousandfold, or manifold, wisdom of God caused people to come from all over the region. The first time Solomon was tested for his wisdom was to settle a dispute between two women. Both of the women were harlots and they both had infant sons. When they went to sleep one of the women rolled over and smothered her child to death. This mother switched her dead child with the child of the other woman. The mother whose child was taken from her woke up and knew the dead child was not hers. The women presented their arguments to King Solomon.

1 Kings 3:23-28

Then said the king, the one said, this *is* my son that lives, and your son *is* the dead: and the other said, No but your son *is* the dead, and my son *is* the living. [24]And the king said, Bring me a sword. And they brought a sword before the king. [25]And the king said, Divide the living child in two, and give half to the one, and half to the other. [26]Then spoke the woman whose the living child *was* unto the king, for her bowels yearned upon her son, and she said, O my lord, give her the living child, and in no wise slay it. But the other said, Let it be neither yours, nor mine *but* divide *it.* [27]Then the king answered and said, Give her the living child, and in no wise slay it: she *is* the mother thereof. [28]And all Israel heard of the judgment that the king had judged; and they feared the king: for they saw that the wisdom of God *was* in him, to do judgment.

Solomon's judgment was a matter of life and death to an innocent baby boy. The case was complicated due to the fact that there were probably no records of birth for the children. The fathers of the children were likely unknown. The two women were known for their unscrupulous affairs and therefore did not carry a lot of credence. There was no undisputable evidence for Solomon to examine, just the word of a prostitute.

Solomon understood that the sword would be the instrument of judgment in the Kingdom. The word of God is represented in the story by a two-edged sword. Solomon's usage of the sword is symbolic of the usage of the word of God. It would be the thousandfold wisdom of God in Solomon that would eventually become an integral part of the word of God.

His decision is used as an example in arbitration and disputes today. The idea of letting go of something you love and it will return to you is founded upon this judgment. This would be the first time that Solomon's thousandfold wisdom would be heard at large. The decision he made that day saved a life and it promoted the platform of his gift to the world. When people heard the details of what Solomon did that day, they were amazed by his wisdom.

From this point on people began to seek Solomon out to hear his wisdom. Thousandfold wisdom is the unlimited measure of God's wisdom. It will magnetically attract people to seek you out and pull on your gift. People are always looking for answers to their problems and wisdom is the solution to all of them. The wisdom of God is the answer to every problem. You may need more money but your answer is not more money, the answer is wisdom because wisdom will produce the path to bring an increase of money into your life.

Beyond the everyday issues of life that everyone goes through, there is always a deep-seated place within the heart of all humans that longs for answers about life and love. Having all the money in the world will not satisfy this longing to know the truth. Wisdom alone can reveal what is hidden deep within. The thousandfold wisdom of Solomon drew leaders of nations to hear his counsel and they came with vast amounts of wealth to give to him for his wisdom.

1 Kings 10:1-3

And when the queen of Sheba heard of the fame of Solomon concerning the name of the LORD, she came to prove him with hard questions. [2]And she came to Jerusalem with a very great train, with camels that bare spices, and very much gold, and precious stones: and when she was come to Solomon, she communed with him of all that was in her heart. [3]And Solomon told her all her questions: there was not *any* thing hid from the king, which he told her not.

The Queen of Sheba came to challenge Solomon's wisdom with hard questions and then Solomon explained all of the queen's questions. The word questions used in verse 1 is the Hebrew word Khee-daw' which means, puzzle, riddle or trick question like a conundrum. Solomon's fame was associated with the name of the Lord Jehovah. Sheba was attempting to undermine the wisdom of Solomon and essentially disprove what she had heard of his fame and to mock the name of the Lord.

1 Kings 10:6-7

And she said to the king, It was a true report that I heard in mine own land of your acts and of your wisdom. [7]Howbeit I believed not the words, until I came, and mine eyes had seen *it*: and, behold, the half was not told me: your wisdom and prosperity exceeds the fame which I heard.

Even though the Queen of Sheba doubted Solomon's wisdom, Solomon's thousandfold wisdom overcame her ridicule by answering the questions of her heart. The word question used in verse 3 is the Hebrew word pronounced daw-bar which means matter, word or thing. The queen was not able to withstand the thousandfold wisdom of Solomon.

The Queen of Sheba approached Solomon in an adversarial position but she left as believer. Remember, her questions were aimed at the validity of the name of the Lord and the thousandfold wisdom given to Solomon. When she saw firsthand how God had blessed Solomon, and those who served him, she was overwhelmed.

1 Kings 10:4-6

And when the queen of Sheba had seen all Solomon's wisdom, and the house that he had built, [5]And the meat of his table, and the sitting of his servants, and the attendance of his ministers, and their apparel, and his cupbearers, and his ascent by which he went up unto the house of the LORD; there was no more spirit in her. [6]And she said to the king, It was a true report that I heard in mine own land of your acts and of your wisdom.

The Queen of Sheba may not have been impressed with the rumors of Solomon's wisdom, but she lost her breath when she saw the prosperity of Solomon's household. Riches and wealth

129

serve as proof of God's wisdom in your life. The wealth and riches in your life is a product of the covenant you have with God.

The wisdom of God can become thousandfold in your life when you use it to build the Kingdom of God. The wisdom that God gave to Solomon produced incredible wealth for both Solomon and the nation of Israel. His thousandfold wisdom produced the thousandfold blessing.

The thousandfold prosperity spoke to the Queen of Sheba and validated God's name and the wisdom that He gave to Solomon. People around you will see the goodness of God when you prosper. This is not for the purpose of show, but as a witness of the presence and prosperity of God in your life.

The Queen of Sheba came to see Solomon with a great deal of her own wealth and riches. She brought wagonloads of gold, precious stones and anointing spices.

1 Kings 10:2a
And she came to Jerusalem with a very great train, with camels that bare spices, and very much gold, and precious stones:

The Queen of Sheba came to give Solomon gifts in exchange for his wisdom. Obviously she is a student of wisdom and it is likely that the wealth that she possessed was the product of the wisdom that she had obtained. She wanted to impress Solomon with her wealth. She brought proper gifts to give to a king.

The wise men of the east brought the same gifts to Jesus when He was a small child. Based on the amount of wealth the Queen of Sheba carried with her and the fact that she was fascinated with the wisdom of Solomon, could be an indication that she may have accumulated her wealth through her own wisdom. Her trip to Israel may have been fueled by her interest in knowing if the Wisdom of Solomon was greater than her own.

1 Kings 10:10
And she gave the king an hundred and twenty talents of gold, and of spices very great store, and precious stones: there came no more such abundance of spices as these which the queen of Sheba gave to king Solomon.

The total weight of the gold that the Queen brought with her was over four and a half tons. That is a total of nine thousand pounds of gold. At today's top price the gold would be worth over 265 million dollars.

She came to see Solomon with a very great train of her own wealth; however, her wealth was just a drop in the bucket compared to Solomon's wealth. The Queen's great train in Hebrew is interpreted to mean "force of wealth." Carrying such a great abundance of wealth was her way of "flexing" her financial muscles.

Money is not the total measure of wealth and riches. Money is the product of wealth. Miracle power and the anointing of God is the true measure of wealth. One of the primary sources of revenue for Sheba was the anointing oil, perfumes and spices they made. The Queen had natural anointing, which produced abundant wealth and riches, but Solomon had supernatural anointing that produced thousandfold wisdom and thousandfold wealth and riches beyond measure.

The Queen of Sheba is known as the "Queen of the South" in the New Testament. Sheba is a mountainous country in southwest Arabia. Sheba developed into a strong commercial power in those days. Its trade specialties were perfumes and incense. Camel caravans followed routes northward across its dry regions, bearing their precious commodities for the royal courts of the countries bordering the Mediterranean Sea.

The Queen came to ask difficult questions but instead Solomon answered the hard questions she could not answer. Afterwards Solomon gave her anything she desired of him. She sowed a wisdom seed with Solomon and reaped a thousandfold return on her seed.

1 Kings 10:13
And king Solomon gave unto the queen of Sheba all her desire, whatsoever she asked, beside *that* which Solomon gave her of his royal bounty. So she turned and went to her own country, she and her servants.

The Queen of Sheba came from an area known as modern day Ethiopia. There is a connection between her and an Ethiopian Treasurer in the New Testament. In the book of Acts there is a story about an Ethiopian Eunuch who met the evangelist Phillip while the Eunuch was reading from the Old Testament book of Isaiah.

Acts 8:26-28
And the angel of the Lord spake unto Philip, saying, Arise, and go toward the south unto the way that goeth down from Jerusalem unto Gaza, which is desert. [27]And he arose and went: and, behold, a man of Ethiopia, an eunuch of great authority under Candace queen of the Ethiopians, who had the charge of

all her treasure, and had come to Jerusalem for to worship, [28] Was returning, and sitting in his chariot read Isaiah the prophet.

It is commonly believed that this Eunuch was a direct descendant of the Queen of Sheba. With that said, it stands to reason that there was a direct connection between the Queen's gifts that she gave to Solomon and the encounter between the eunuch with Phillip. This eunuch was the treasurer over the entire wealth of the nation of Ethiopia. A eunuch is a male that has been castrated so that he has no desire for sexual relations, or has been born as such and therefore can be trusted to watch over a harem of women for a king or leader. Jesus talked about Kingdom eunuchs in the book of Matthew.

Matthew 19:12
For there are some eunuchs, which were so born from *their* mother's womb: and there are some eunuchs, which were made eunuchs of men: and there be eunuchs, which have made themselves eunuchs for the kingdom of heaven's sake. He that is able to receive *it*, let him receive *it*.

Some believers decide to become a Kingdom eunuch for the Lord. They have cut themselves off from the things of the flesh so that they can be consecrated to God. Anna, the prophetess, is a great example of a Kingdom eunuch. I believe that every Christian should become a Kingdom eunuch in regard to finances.

If we view the money that God empowers us to handle as His money, He will trust us with greater amounts of money and more importantly, He will trust us with true riches. True riches are the anointing. True riches release the miraculous ability of

133

God. True riches are the highest form of riches and it is dealt to you according to your faithfulness with natural riches.

This eunuch is a Jewish man on his way to worship Jehovah in Jerusalem. Jerusalem was the same place that the Queen of Sheba met with Solomon. Philip was sent by the Lord to speak specifically to this man. This was no chance encounter, it was God appointed.

Acts 8:29-30

Then the Spirit said unto Philip, Go near, and join yourself to this chariot. [30]And Philip ran thither to *him*, and heard him read the prophet Isaiah, and said, do you understand what you read?

Philip was sent by God to interpret the scriptures for the eunuch so that the eunuch could receive Jesus as Savior and Lord and so the Gospel could go back to Ethiopia.

Acts 8:29-35

Then the Spirit said unto Philip, Go near, and join yourself to this chariot. [30]And Philip ran thither to *him*, and heard him read the prophet Isaiah, and said, Understand you what you read? [31]And he said, How can I, except some man should guide me? And he desired Philip that he would come up and sit with him. [32] The place of the scripture which he read was this, He was led as a sheep to the slaughter; and like a lamb dumb before his shearer, so opened he not his mouth: [33]In his humiliation his judgment was taken away: and who shall declare his generation? for his life is taken from the earth. [34]And the eunuch answered Philip, and said, I pray you, of whom speaks the prophet this? of himself, or of some other man? [35]Then Philip opened his mouth, and began at the same scripture, and preached unto him Jesus.

When the Queen of Sheba returned home, she must have converted to Judaism because the nation followed Jehovah instead of the pagan gods they worshipped. Her experience with Solomon and his thousandfold wisdom changed her life forever and apparently changed the people of Ethiopia for many years to follow.

Acts 8:36-38

And as they went on *their* way, they came unto a certain water: and the eunuch said, See, *here is* water; what does hinder me to be baptized? [37]And Philip said, If you believe with all your heart, you may. And he answered and said, I believe that Jesus Christ is the Son of God. [38]And he commanded the chariot to stand still: and they went down both into the water, both Philip and the eunuch; and he baptized him.

This man was both a eunuch and a treasurer. This parallel description of this man speaks of his character as to being trustworthy. He was trustworthy with another person's possessions and wealth. Jesus said that if you cannot be trusted with another man's wealth, who will trust you with true riches?

The truest riches in the world is the truth of God's word. This eunuch was the recipient of the harvest of the seed of the word of God, and was selected by God to return the Gospel to the same nation that the Queen of Sheba had brought back the thousandfold Wisdom of Solomon. Her abundant seed sown with Solomon became the abundant harvest of salvation for her family one thousand years later!

Solomon took the throne of Israel in 970 B.C. and he reigned for 40 years as the King of Israel. From 970 B.C. until the inception of the ministry of Jesus in 30 A.D. was exactly

1000 years. God measured one thousand years between the reign of King Solomon and the reign of the King of all kings, Jesus. This would set up the beginning of the eternal promise that God made to King David concerning the establishment of a king that would always be on the Throne of David. The thousandfold principle is in full force here.

The seed that the Queen of Sheba sowed with King Solomon a thousand years earlier had now come to full maturity and has produced the fruit of salvation for the nation of Ethiopia through Jesus. Philip's obedience to the voice of the Holy Spirit to go towards Jerusalem brought this thousandfold seed full circle.

Acts 8:39-40
And when they were come up out of the water, the Spirit of the Lord caught away Philip, that the eunuch saw him no more: and he went on his way rejoicing. [40]But Philip was found at Azotus: and passing through he preached in all the cities, till he came to Caesarea.

The effect of the thousandfold principle is so powerful that after Philip baptizes the Ethiopian Eunuch in water, the Spirit of God translated the physical body of Philip from Jerusalem to Azotus. The thousandfold anointing took Philip to a whole new spiritual level.

Thousandfold wisdom is the product of a thousandfold seed. The power and anointing of the thousandfold will transcend time and the generations to bring the promises of God to pass in your lifetime and in the life of your descendants. When you flow in the power of the thousandfold wisdom you will see family salvation and the preaching of the word of God to the nations of the world.

The greatest thing about the thousandfold wisdom is the fact that it releases unlimited measure and ability to answer all of the difficult questions you may have, and it will bring incredible financial rewards as well.

Chapter 8
Thousandfold Faith

There is a direct connection between giving by the thousands and unlocking the door to the unlimited favor and blessing of God. But what if you are not able to give a thousand dollars, pounds or any other standard of money? Can you give less money and still get the same results? The answer is yes, with conditions.

When Solomon gave one thousand burnt offerings before God, he took them to the top of the high hill of Gibeon to sacrifice them on an altar to God. Gibeon was the location that people were making sacrifices atop at that time. Bringing a sacrifice to the top of the hill required an extra effort. Solomon walked one thousand animals up the side of Gibeon. That is a lot of work no matter how you slice it.

It was not an easy task for him. I am an avid golfer, and I like to walk the golf course instead of riding in an electric cart. There are some places in the course where I have to pull the golf bag up a hill and it takes a lot out of me to get to the top. When I reach the top of the hill I am climbing, I generally stop and get my breath before I continue with my next golf shot. Walking this way conditions me physically to walk all 18 holes and play a better round of golf.

When Solomon walked up and down Gibeon, it would have conditioned him to give to God consistently and with a purpose. He did the same thing over and over again one thousand times with expectation of a visitation from God. Many people give up on sowing and reaping because they do not see instant results.

They grow weary of giving to God and quickly blame the messengers that instructed them on how to give and receive. Giving consistently will condition you to develop a greater expectation of your faith. You should give to God consistently from the heart, when you give this way you will not become indifferent and lose heart.

Galatians 6:9-10

And let us not be weary in well doing: for in due season we shall reap, if we faint not. [10]As we have therefore opportunity, let us do good unto all *men*, especially unto them who are of the household of faith.

Sowing and reaping is a Kingdom principle of increase that will always work for the persistently faithful. It may seem monotonous to bring the tithes and offerings to the Lord, but if you give it with understanding the word of God promises that you will reap incredible benefits. You may not always feel like giving for one reason or another, but The Apostle Paul referred to it as being "instant in season or out of season." In other words, be ready to give when it is convenient and when it is not.

Solomon walked a thousand animals up the high hill of Gibeon. He did not hire someone to do this for him. Solomon could have commanded his servants to take the thousandfold offering to Gibeon but he did not. When you give to God, it is important that you understand the correlation between what comes from your hand and what comes from your heart. God loves a cheerful giver whose heart is in their giving.

Solomon must have had a tremendous amount of physical stamina and immense will spiritually to do this one thousand times in a row. The same principle applies to your sacrifices to the Lord. If the gifts you bring to the Lord do not take you higher and expend your effort to get there then it does not qualify as a thousandfold offering. In other words, if the gift you offer to God does not represent a sacrifice from your life, it will not qualify as a thousandfold gift. King David said it best when he bought the threshing floor from Araunah.

2 Samuel 24:22-24

And Araunah said unto David, Let my lord the king take and offer up what *seems* good unto him: behold, *here be* oxen for burnt sacrifice, and threshing instruments and *other* instruments of the oxen for wood. [23]All these *things* did Araunah, *as* a king, give unto the king. And Araunah said unto the king, The LORD your God accept you. [24]And the king said unto Araunah, No; but I will surely buy *it* of you at a price: neither will I offer burnt offerings unto the LORD my God of that which does cost me nothing. So David bought the threshing floor and the oxen for fifty shekels of silver.

If you pay nothing for something that is what you will probably think it is worth. If you don't pay the price to obtain something, you will never appreciate its true value. David said that he would not present an offering unto God that he did not feel. If your gift moves you, it will move God but if it doesn't move you, it likely will not move God either.

When David bought the threshing floor, he was looking for a place to make a sacrificial offering that would cause God to be entreated and stop the plague over the nation that had killed 70,000 men. In other words, this would be no ordinary offering in size or purpose. David did three things that day that changed the future forever:

- He bought the ground on which the sacrifice was offered.
- He built the altar for the sacrifice to lay upon the altar.
- He burnt the sacrifice as a peace offering unto God.

This story played a vital role in securing the real estate for the Temple of God. It became the land that Solomon built the Temple upon and it ultimately will become the site for the eternal Temple where Jesus will sit upon His throne as the King of kings and the Lord of lords. This real estate would become the location of the place where the thousandfold Kingdom of God would seat Jesus as the King of kings.

This was certainly a defining moment in history and a critical moment for the nation of Israel as well. The 70,000 men died as a result of David's disobedience to God. The reason that these men died was because David conducted a census of the people against God's will and the advice of his military leader, Joab.

David wanted to arrive at a finite number of the households in the nation. Joab advised him not to do it because he was already hundredfold. The devil rose up against David and tempted him to make the census. You may notice that the account is recorded in both 2 Samuel and 1 Chronicles. In 2 Samuel the Bible says the lord stood up and tempted David, this is not speaking of the Lord our God, this is speaking of satan. In 1 Chronicles the Bible says that satan stood up against David. God does not tempt anyone nor can He be tempted.

Why did the people die if it wasn't their fault? Good question. God did not want David to number the people because He made a promise to Abraham that his seed would be without number like the stars of the heavens, sand of the seashore and the dust of the earth. Counting the people was an attempt to place a finite number on the promise God gave to Abraham. The devil's provoking became David's pride. Joab understood the dilemma and that is why he tried to stop David from this terrible tragedy.

David disregarded the counsel of Joab, his trusted military commander, and ordered the census to fuel his ego. This disobedience opened the door for the enemy to come in. Pestilence came upon the people and 70,000 innocent men died.

When David saw the death angel move across the land, he went to the prophet Gad for counsel. Gad sought the Lord and David was given three choices of punishment for the sin he committed. He chose the punishment of falling into the hand of the Lord; for His mercies are great. David wanted to take personal responsibility and stop the plague from killing any more men.

2 Samuel 24:24b & 25
...So David bought the threshing floor and the oxen for fifty shekels of silver. [25]And David built there an altar unto the LORD, and offered burnt offerings and peace offerings. So the LORD was entreated for the land, and the plague was stayed from Israel.

David purchased the threshing floor and the oxen for the sacrifice to God from Araunah. The plague ceased because God accepted the gift from David and the Lord stopped the plague.

David's attempt to bring a fixed number on the nation placed a limit on the growth factor because it contradicted God's promise to Abraham. God told Abraham that his seed would be innumerable. Any attempt to place a finite number on the people would be considered a challenge to God's promise. The promise to Abraham was that his seed would be unlimited in measure.

Any attempt to place a limitation on population growth will be met with judgment. Planned Parenthood and other murderous abortion mills like them are part of the reasons that there are so many plagues and pestilences consuming lives around the world. Euthanasia, homosexuality and abortion are all demonic plans to steal, kill and destroy lives.

The devil is opposed to God and wants to hinder the advancement of the seed of Abraham. Christians are the seed of Abraham by faith through the blood of Jesus. The devil wants to kill, steal and destroy anyone that has the anointing and blessing of God upon them.

The thousandfold principle is a force from Heaven that thrusts the engine of life through the generations. It causes everything it touches to be fruitful and multiply. Moses spoke over the nation of Israel that they would be a thousand times greater than they were. God's word gives us the same provision and power.

The thousandfold principle is a life principle, not just a financial one. Everything about the Kingdom of God is based upon, and operates on, the thousandfold principle. God's people can see thousandfold result in every aspect of their lives.

Any Christian can partake in the thousandfold principle, even if they do not have a thousand dollars or a thousand measures to give. There are times and situations where the thousandfold faith kicks in for those who have very little amounts to give to the Lord.

Remember, God blesses the measure not the amount. If the gifts you bring to the Lord do not take you higher and expend your effort to get there then it does not qualify as a thousandfold offering. If they do, then your gift will qualify as a thousandfold seed.

Here are a few examples of people in the Bible who proved the thousandfold principle in their lives by giving everything that they had to give:

- The widow of Sarephath gave her last meal to Elijah and ate for many days after and her supplies never dried up nor ran out.
- The widow's two mites in the offering was called by Jesus, bigger than all those who gave collectively.
- The woman with the alabaster box gave a lifetime memorial seed and her gift releases an anointing aroma every time the gospel is preached. Jesus said she gave what she could.
- The boy who gave his five loaves and two fish. That was his maximum measure. The Lord multiplied the thousandfold gift by feeding 5,000 and in another instance 4,000.

When you give at maximum measure then God returns with His unlimited measure. A measure to God is one thousand. When God multiplies your maximum measure, He measures back by thousandfold measure. God measures things out by the thousands. When the prophet Ezekiel saw the vision of the Temple he specifically noted that when God measured the Temple, He used the number one thousand as the standard of measure.

Ezekiel 47:3-5

And when the man that had the line in his hand went forth eastward, **he measured a thousand** cubits, and he brought me through the waters; the waters *were* to the ankles. [4]Again **he measured a thousand**, and brought me through the waters; the waters *were* to the knees. Again **he measured a thousand**, and brought me through; the waters *were* to the loins. [5]Afterward **he measured a thousand**; *and it was* a river that I could not pass over: for the waters were risen, waters to swim in, a river that could not be passed over.

There are many people around the world that only make a couple of dollars a day. Finding a thousand dollars or a thousand anything to give to God may be extremely difficult. The thousandfold principle is based upon the measure, not the amount.

When someone gives a maximum measure to God, they are extending thousandfold faith in God's ability to return the seed with an increase. This only applies to the situation where the individual is not in a position to give a thousand but they give everything they can.

When Abraham was challenged by God to offer Isaac, his only son of promise, in sacrifice to Him it would require giving his maximum measure. Abraham was fully persuaded that God would resurrect Isaac if he died on Mt. Moriah. This event opened the door for God to offer Jesus as His only begotten Son on the cross of Calvary. Jesus was God's maximum measure or thousandfold offering for all mankind.

Solomon was in a position to give a thousandfold offering. Solomon gave a thousand measures when he offered the thousand animals before God. From what I have studied, I believe that it was very likely that the animals that Solomon gave to God were oxen. At today's prices 1,000 oxen would amount to over 2 million U.S. dollars. The gifts that came from Solomon were conducive to his ability to give. Jesus said, "To whom much is given, much is required." Little is much when it costs you something.

- $1,000 is one thousand U.S. dollar bills.
- $100 is one thousand U.S. dimes.
- $10 is one thousand U.S. pennies.

Each one of these qualifies for the thousandfold giving principle depending on your given situation. As long as you know you have "done what you could", the gift becomes a sacrifice.

When the budget is tight we often say, "Sacrifices are going to have to be made." We are led to believe that a sacrifice is a cut back on expenses. But in the Kingdom of God a sacrifice means so much more. A sacrifice to God is the act of giving something valued for the sake of honoring God as more important, or worthy, in our life. You don't hear the word sacrifice used in this text much any more.

Unfortunately people tend to pull back on their giving when the economy turns down or they lose their job. The natural knee-jerk reaction of the flesh is to hold on instead of letting go. The response of the spiritual person is to continue giving at the same level or even increasing their gifts to combat the recession, inflation or economic disaster.

There is an old saying in business that goes like this, "When things are good you should advertise, when things are bad you must." The same rule applies in giving and receiving to God. In good times you should always give to God, but in bad times you must.

This requires real thousandfold faith in order to execute the principle successfully. Real thousandfold faith does not pay regard to its circumstances, it overcomes them. Abraham was a man of strong faith, so was his wife Sarah.

Romans 4:19-21
And being not weak in faith, he considered not his own body now dead, when he was about an hundred years old, neither yet the deadness of Sara's womb: [20] He staggered not at the promise of God through unbelief; but was strong in faith, giving glory to God; [21]And being fully persuaded that, what he had promised, he was able also to perform.

Abraham and Sarah were well past the time of life for bearing children by medical standard, but not by Kingdom standards. God promised and Abraham knew that he was able to perform His promise. We don't perform the miracle, we believe the one who does.

Abraham and Sarah chose to believe God's word and to stay in faith. They did not deny the facts; they overcame them by believing the truth. The truth always overcomes the facts. No matter what the report of the world is, you must choose to believe the report of the Lord. When you need a money miracle you must hold on to your faith and let go of your seed, not the opposite.

When God told Abraham he was going to have a son, Abraham fell on his face laughing. When God told Sarah that she was going to have a baby boy, she laughed inwardly. They

148

did conceive and brought forth Isaac. Isaac's name means laughter. The outward laughter of Abraham was the seed of faith that caused the inward laughter of Sarah's faith to combine and become the promised son Isaac.

Thousandfold faith is empowered by the strength of God to accomplish things we cannot do in our own strength. Nehemiah said the joy of the Lord is our strength. The laughter and joy of Abraham and Sarah produced the strength to bring forth Isaac into the world. We should give cheerfully and willing when we give to God and especially when we give in the thousandfold levels.

God told Abraham that He had already made him a father of many nations even before Isaac and Ishmael were born. When God says a thing it is established as if it were complete and manifested. God told Sarah that she would become the mother of nations and kings would come forth from her womb.

This is a thousandfold confession. You should make the same confession over the womb of your spirit. You should say that you have favor with God and man. Say that you have covenant wealth and health. Say that your family is saved and set free from bondage and addiction. Say that you have a surplus of prosperity and a super abundance of provision. Make your confession regardless of your situation. Overcome the obstacles by using your overcoming faith to leap over them.

The thouandfold principle must be adjoined to your thousandfold faith confession. Once you have sown a thousandfold seed, keep your thousandfold faith watering the seed you have planted. The Lord of the Harvest will take over from there.

Isaac was the product of God's promise of the thousandfold faith exercised by his parents. Isaac was the one thing they wanted more then anything in life. I am sure there are some things that you desire to take place with great passion. Passion is the fuel that empowers your dreams even when it seems that they have stalled.

Isaac met his dream girl in Rebekah. Rebekah was a beautiful woman with a servant's heart. When Abraham's servant discovered her, he pronounced the thousandfold blessing upon her because she gave water to him and his animals.

Genesis 24:60
And they blessed Rebekah, and said unto her, You *art* our sister, be you *the mother* of thousands of millions, and let your seed possess the gate of those which hate them.

This is the only scripture in the entire Bible where the word million is utilized. This verse says thousands in plural and millions in plural. A thousand times a million is a billion. Thousands times millions equals billions.

Today we have over 6.8 billion souls on the planet and growing every second. To reach them we must have the tools necessary to teach the word and preach the gospel, so that they may have a chance to hear the good news about the love of God and His merciful plan of salvation.

The Body of Christ must wake up and see the need to becoming rich and wealthy for the Kingdom of God so that we can obtain the tools necessary to preach the Gospel. Billions of lost souls are dependent on it.

I know there are assortments of naysayers that do not believe this and some that make it their life's goal to combat it under the cover of Christianity. They propagate a message of anti-prosperity in an attempt to box in and contain them. They are broken cisterns, wells without water. The Apostle Paul said it best.

2 Timothy 3:5
Having a form of godliness, but denying the power thereof: from such turn away.

2 Timothy 3:7
Ever learning, and never able to come to the knowledge of the truth.

I suggest you part company with anyone that opposes prosperity in the Kingdom of God and take hold of the promises of God that bless you and multiply you for His glory. God told Abraham that through him all families of the earth would be blessed. This is the very definition of the Gospel.

Galatians 3:8-9
And the scripture, foreseeing that God would justify the heathen through faith, preached before the gospel unto Abraham, *saying*, In you shall all nations be blessed. [9]So then they which are of faith are blessed with faithful Abraham.

The Gospel was preached to Abraham before Jesus ever appeared on the planet. It has always been God's intentions for us to be blessed and empowered by His anointing to have covenant wealth, health and peace. Under the Adamic curse we can never have these things but we have been redeemed from the curse of the law through Christ Jesus our Lord and Savior and have a responsibility and a right to get them.

Until you open up your heart and mind to the thousandfold principle of the word of God, you will not see how immense the measure of supply and provision you have access to. Thousandfold faith is immeasurable, infinite and unbounded in its potential.

The only thing that prevents the thousandfold from working is your lack of faith and willingness to accept it. In the Day of Judgment believers will not be judged for sin. We will face judgment for the works we have done as a born-again believer.

The bases of rewards are found in the book of Matthew.

<u>Matthew 25:14-30</u>

For *the kingdom of heaven is* as a man travelling into a far country, *who* called his own servants, and delivered unto them his goods. [15]And unto one he gave five talents, to another two, and to another one; to every man according to his several ability; and straightway took his journey. [16]Then he that had received the five talents went and traded with the same, and made *them* other five talents. [17]And likewise he that *had received* two, he also gained other two. [18]But he that had received one went and dug in the earth, and hid his lord's money. [19]After a long time the lord of those servants come, and reckon with them. [20]And so he that had received five talents came and brought other five talents, saying, Lord, You delivered unto me five talents: behold, I have gained beside them five talents more. [21] His lord said unto him, Well done, *you* good and faithful servant: you have been faithful over a few things, I will make you ruler over many things: enter you into the joy of your lord. [22] He also that had received two talents came and said, Lord, you delivered unto me two talents: behold, I have gained two other talents beside them. [23]His lord said unto him, Well done, good and faithful servant; you have been faithful over a few things, I will make you ruler over many things: enter you into the joy of your lord. [24]Then he which had received the one talent came and said, Lord, I knew you that you are a hard man, reaping where you have not sown, and gathering where you have not sown: [25]And I was afraid, and went and hid your talent in the earth: lo, *there* you have *that is* yours. [26] His lord answered and said unto him, *You* wicked and slothful servant, you knew that I reap where I sowed not, and gather where I have not sown: [27]You ought therefore to have put my money to the exchangers, and *then* at my coming I should have received mine own with usury. [28]Take therefore the talent from him, and give *it* unto him which has ten talents. [29]For unto every one that has shall be given, and he shall have abundance: but from him that has not shall be taken away even that which he has. [30]And cast you the unprofitable servant into outer darkness: there shall be weeping and gnashing of teeth.

Jesus demonstrates through this allegory that the rewards for a Christian are given to us based on the way we handle money. Talents are a standard of currency, not the ability to play the piano well. In the parable, three men receive the opportunity to multiply their lord's money. When the lord of these servants shows up, two of the servants turned a profit for him but the third one did not.

The first man doubled the money from five talents into ten talents. The second man doubled the money from two talents into four talents. So both of these men operated at the same level of faith producing the same results in double measure. Remember, God acknowledges increase by the measure.

The third man was a mess. Because of fear he hid the money in a napkin.

Luke 19:20
And another came, saying, Lord, behold, *here is* your pound, which I have kept laid up in a napkin:

Napkin is the Greek word sudarium. A sudarium is a sweat cloth. A sweat cloth was used in that day to wrap the face of the dead. Lazarus had a sweat cloth on his face when he came back from the dead. Jesus commanded that his grave clothes be removed including the sudarium. Jesus had a sweat cloth, or napkin, around his face when He was laid in the tomb but He left it in the tomb so we would never have to wear one.

The third man's fear caused him to hide his master's money and gain nothing in trading. When the lord of the servants addresses them, he rewards them based on their achievements. The napkin symbolizes death and in this case death over the money he was trusted with. This man's fear and lack of understanding caused the money that he was trusted with to be buried in him.

When we keep the tithes and offerings we are robbing God and ourselves. This is an act of the flesh that came from the dust of the earth. When we hide the things that belong to God in our self, we invite the seedeater to devour them.

Malachi 3:10-11
Bring you all the tithes into the storehouse, that there may be meat in mine house, and prove me now here with, says the

LORD of hosts, if I will not open you the windows of heaven, and pour you out a blessing, that *there shall* not *be room* enough *to receive it.* [11]And I will rebuke the devourer for your sakes, and he shall not destroy the fruits of your ground; neither shall your vine cast her fruit before the time in the field, says the LORD of hosts.

In the Garden of Eden, satan is the seedeater that was cursed to crawl on his belly and eat the dust of the ground.

Genesis 3:14
And the LORD God said unto the serpent, Because you have done this, you *are* cursed above all cattle, and above every beast of the field; upon your belly shall you go, and dust shall you eat all the days of your life:

When you keep the money that belongs to God to yourself, you invite satan to devour it. He devours the money you hide in a napkin. The thousandfold principle can never take effect for you if you keep money hidden from the Kingdom of God.

God takes pleasure in three things:
- Your **RELATIONSHIP** with Him. Matthew 3:17 (My son in whom I am well pleased).
- Your **FAITH** in Him. Hebrews 11:6 (Without faith it is impossible to please Him).
- Your **PROSPERITY**. Psalm 35:27 (He takes pleasure in the prosperity of his servants).

God does not take pleasure in the soul that draws back.

Hebrews 10:38
Now the just shall live by faith: but if any man draw back, my soul shall have no pleasure in him.

It displeases God when we don't believe Him and when we draw back from the faith He gave us. Many people look for perfect conditions to sow in. There is no such thing.

Ecclesiastes 11:4-6   The Living Bible

If you wait for perfect conditions, you will never get anything done. [5]God's ways are as mysterious as the pathway of the wind and as the manner in which a human spirit is infused into the little body of a baby while it is yet in its mother's womb. [6]Keep on sowing your seed, for you never know which will grow, perhaps it all will.

Drought and famine can be good conditions for your miracle.   Sowing during difficult times can activate the thousandfold principle. You are standing on miracle soil when the conditions aren't conducive and the odds are against you. You will never have a better opportunity to test the waters of the thousandfold principle. The thousandfold promise to God's people is that we will laugh at drought and famine because it cannot prevent the blessing of God on our life.

Job 5:20-22

In famine he shall redeem you from death: and in war from the power of the sword. [21]You shall be hid from the scourge of the tongue: neither shall you be afraid of destruction when it comes. [22]At destruction and famine you shall laugh: neither shall you be afraid of the beasts of the earth.

Thousandfold faith is the unlimited measure of faith that opens the flow of God's unlimited power, anointing and ability in your life. Giving in thousandfold measure permits God to reciprocate in thousandfold return.

156

Every person is dealt the measure of faith. That measure can manifest anything the word of God says you can have, do or be. The measure of faith can bring forth anything on the earth in hundredfold measure. You have a finite measure of faith but God does not. God has unlimited, or thousandfold, faith. You can operate with your faith in God's word and you can operate with God's faith too.

Jesus said that we could have the "God kind of faith" in Mark's Gospel Chapter 11.

Mark 11:22
And Jesus answering said unto them, have faith in God.

This is interpreted to mean that you can have God's faith. Jesus said this to the disciples after he cursed the fig tree. He wanted you to know that you can do the same things God can do with His thousandfold faith. Jesus was saying that you could operate in a level of faith that God uses and have the same results God does. There is nothing too hard for God and nothing impossible for you. When you tap into the thousandfold faith of God there is no limit to what you can do!

157

Chapter 9
Thousandfold Prosperity

Psalm 144:13

That our garners *may be* full, affording all manner of store: *that* our sheep may bring forth thousands and ten thousands in our streets:

David prayed that the Lord would multiply the people's possession by thousandfold measure. The thousandfold principle is a force of power that will multiply your money, career, savings, investments and any possession you are a steward over. The thousandfold principle is God's unlimited power and ability to operate in every aspect of your life. The thousandfold principle holds the potential to unleash unlimited amounts of riches and wealth for you.

When Solomon gave to God at Gibeon his objective was to gain the wisdom, or supernatural intelligence, of God to rule the nation and to construct the Temple that his father David designed and longed to build. God gave Solomon wisdom and much more than he asked for. In addition to wisdom God gave him riches and honor. God declared that there would never be a king as wealthy as Solomon on the earth. Only Jesus would be greater.

Solomon used this wisdom for the purpose of building the Temple. The Temple was a spectacular edifice made from extremely expensive materials, including rare gold called the gold of ophir and other precious metals and materials that came to Solomon through the favor and blessing of God.

159

The wisdom, favor and blessing of God produced incredible ability for Solomon to negotiate for the materials and workman to build the Temple for the glory of God. That does not take into account the priceless value of the sentimental and religious significance the Temple brought to the people.

It was an architectural achievement of monumental proportions. The project was the lifelong vision of King David that came from his desire to build a house for God to dwell in among humans on the earth.

2 Samuel 7:1-6

And it came to pass, when the king sat in his house, and the LORD had given him rest round about from all his enemies; ^{2}That the king said unto Nathan the prophet, See now, I dwell in an house of cedar, but the ark of God dwells within curtains. ^{3}And Nathan said to the king, Go, do all that *is* in your heart; for the LORD *is* with you. ^{4}And it came to pass that night, that the word of the LORD came unto Nathan, saying, ^{5}Go and tell my servant David, Thus says the LORD, Shall you build me an house for me to dwell in? ^{6}Whereas I have not dwelt in *any* house since the time that I brought up the children of Israel out of Egypt, even to this day, but have walked in a tent and in a tabernacle.

David wanted a house for God to dwell in like He dwelt with Israel in the wilderness in the Tabernacle of Moses. David wanted to build a structure that brought glory and honor to God. David often communicated with God through a prophet. The prophet Nathan told David to do what he wanted with all his heart; but afterwards God told Nathan to go and tell David I am pleased to dwell in tents and because he was willing to build a dwelling place for God, I will build you a house.

The tents God is speaking of are the tabernacles, or tents, of mankind. The Apostle Paul said that you are the Temple of the Holy Ghost. That is to say that you are the tent that God inhabits.

1 Corinthians 6:19-20

What? know you not that your body is the temple of the Holy Ghost *which is* in you, which you have of God, and you are not your own? [20]For you are bought with a price: therefore glorify God in your body, and in your spirit, which are God's.

The principle of first mention is applied in this instance. In order for God to legally operate or do anything on the earth, He must do so through humans. This is because God gave the original authority and dominion to Adam in the Garden of Eden. God would violate His own word if he bypassed mankind and usurped the authority he gave to man. David opened the door for God to send His son Jesus as the ultimate Temple for mankind. Jesus entered into the world the legal way, through the womb of a woman.

Galatians 4:4-5

But when the fullness of the time was come, God sent forth his Son, made of a woman, made under the law, [5]To redeem them that were under the law, that we might receive the adoption of sons.

John 1:14

And the Word was made flesh, and dwelt among us, (and we beheld his glory, the glory as of the only begotten of the Father,) full of grace and truth.

161

John 10:9-10

I am the door: by me if any man enter in, he shall be saved, and shall go in and out, and find pasture. [10]The thief cometh not, but for to steal, and to kill, and to destroy: I am come that they might have life, and that they might have *it* more abundantly.

The Law of First Mention states that whenever a man does something first on the earth it establishes the standard from that point on. When people did things in the Bible they would often open the door between heaven and earth for God to intervene. Here are some examples of the Law of First Mention that opened doors for us:

- Abraham opened the door of faith.
- Abraham paid tithes of all so God could send perpetual communion and blessing.
- Abraham offered Isaac and God sent Jesus to be His offering.
- Jacob vowed to be a tither so God would keep His promise with us.
- Joseph was imprisoned wrongfully so Jesus could be imprisoned for us.
- Job became sick and poor so that Jesus could take our sickness and through His poverty we might be made rich.
- David determined to build a house for God so God could build a house for us.
- Solomon sowed 1,000 sacrifices so that God could release the thousandfold blessing on us.

God made a promise to build a permanent dwelling place for all that call upon the name of the Lord Jesus. These promises allowed God to set up the location of the throne that Jesus will eternally be seated upon to reign and rule forever and ever.

162

2 Samuel 7:11-13
And as since the time that I commanded judges *to be* over my people Israel, and have caused you to rest from all your enemies. Also the LORD tells me that he will make me an house. [12]And when your days be fulfilled, and you shall sleep with your fathers, I will set up your seed after you, which shall proceed out of your bowels, and I will establish his kingdom. [13]He shall build an house for my name, and I will establish the throne of his kingdom for ever.

David wanted to build a permanent dwelling place for the Ark of the Covenant. Before this point the Ark of the Covenant was placed in the Tabernacle of Moses. In Shiloh the Philistines defeated Israel in battle and took the Tabernacle of Moses and its contents with them. David retrieved the Ark and returned it back to the city of Jerusalem. David ordered the Ark be placed in a tent for the purpose of worship when they brought the Ark back into the city.

This tent is known as the Tabernacle of David. This tent was a transitional tabernacle designed to enclose the Ark of the Covenant until the Temple was built. The Ark rested on the same location as the site for the Temple of Solomon. This piece of ground is the place where the modern day Dome of the Rock is built in Jerusalem. The Jews believe this is the sacred location of both the Temple of Solomon and Herod's Temple.

Furthermore, the Jews believe that this is where Abraham brought Isaac to offer him in sacrifice to God. If that is true, then it should be noted that Jacob dreamed about the ladder in Genesis 28 at the same place. To say the least, the site serves a significant part of the Hebrew and Christian history, as well as the future of the world.

David spared no expense for the materials to build the Temple of Solomon. An immense amount of costly materials were used to build the Temple of Solomon. David was a valiant warrior and was known as the champion of Israel after beating Goliath in battle. David had defeated all of his enemies round about him and spoiled all of their goods. His victories produced incredible amounts of wealth and riches for him, the nation and for the Kingdom of God.

David was known as a man after God's own heart. God chose David to be the King of Israel and God honored David for his character and willingness to walk in integrity. David had many victories in his life, but he also knew what trouble was and what God would do in the midst of trouble and distress. The distress that David encountered would serve as the vehicle of prosperity and increase for him. Distress can serve a purpose in your life. Distress will bring incredible prosperity for you. David knew that distress acted as a platform for increase.

Psalm 4:1
Hear me when I call, O God of my righteousness: you have enlarged me *when I was* in distress; have mercy upon me, and hear my prayer.

The enlargement of David's prosperity amassed a tremendous fortune. David made it clear that the reason that God enlarged his wealth was for the preparation of the building of the Temple.

1 Chronicles 22:14-16
Now, behold, in my trouble I have prepared for the house of the LORD an hundred **thousand** talents of gold, and a **thousand thousand** talents of silver; and of brass and iron without weight;

for it is in abundance: timber also and stone have I prepared; and you may add thereto. [15]Moreover *there are* workmen with you in abundance, hewers and workers of stone and timber, and all manner of cunning men for every manner of work. [16]Of the gold, the silver, and the brass, and the iron, *there is* no number. Arise *therefore*, and be doing, and the LORD be with you.

It was the distress and trouble that David was all too familiar with that helped him to collect the gold and materials needed to build Solomon's Temple. David also learned how to reign and rule while going through the problems. When David was hiding from Saul he became a captain over four hundred men that were in distress, in debt and in discontentment in a cave called Adullam. David brought these men out of the cave and into a wealthy place. They learned from David how to take charge of their lives in a difficult setting. You must learn how to rule in your circumstance before you can come out into your wealthy place and dominate in your finances.

Many people think that when things settle down and the pressure comes off that they will commence prospering. David affirmed that his ability to accumulate the wealth he designated for the building of the Temple was a result of the problems and pressures that came against him. God does not give you the problems and pressures, but He will use them as instruments of reward for your faithfulness. He will expand your horizons and extend your life through them.

Notice in 1 Chronicles Chapter 22 that the gold and the silver are both measured by the thousands. It was one hundred thousand talents of gold and one thousand thousands, or one million talents of silver. The gold and silver that David prepared for the House of God is weighed and measured by the thousands. Prosperity in the Kingdom of God comes in thousandfold measure.

David brought 100,000 talents of gold and 1 million talents of silver for building materials of the Temple of Solomon. A talent of gold in the Bible is equal to approximately 94 pounds. There are 16 ounces in a pound so 16 times 94 = 1504 ounces. The gold used in the Temple was known as the gold of Ophir (O-feer). Today no one knows where this gold came from or where it can be found. Because of its purity and rarity the price of Ophir gold would net the highest possible value of all gold known to mankind, not to exclude the genuine value it represents spiritually.

The highest form of gold traded on the market today is called Platinum American Eagle Gold. As of this writing it was traded for $1,840.30 per ounce. So for examples sake, let's use this gold price as the multiplier of the 100,000 talents of gold David collected through his spoils of war. It would look like this in our current dollar standard:

100,000 talents x 94 pounds x 16 ounces = 150,400,000 ounces of gold.

150,400,000 ounces of gold x $1,840.30 gold price per ounce = $276,781,120,000.00

That is two hundred seventy six billion, seven hundred eighty one million, one hundred twenty thousand dollars and no cents. That is just the gold price alone. The silver is measured as a thousand times a thousand, or a million talents. Silver is sold today at $18.40 per ounce. The silver in the offering brought by

David for the Temple of Solomon would look like this in our current dollar standard:

1,000,000,000 talents x 94 pounds x 16 ounces = 1,504,000,000 ounces of silver x $18.40 per ounce = $27,673,600,000.00

That is twenty seven billion, six hundred seventy three million, six hundred thousand dollars and no cents. That is just over ten percent of the gold value. I would dare say that there are no church buildings or facilities on the earth today that are appraised even near the price of the silver in the Temple of Solomon not to mention the gold. Just imagine the headlines in the news if a ministry were to build such a lavish facility for the purpose of worshipping and sacrificing to God. It would be the top story on every news agency, the subject of blogging all over the Internet.

A thousandfold thinker does not flinch at the thousandfold principle and are not moved by the opinions of the world. They understand the purpose of prosperity and are not ashamed of it. After all, God uses silver, gold and precious stones to build entire cities in Heaven. Why shouldn't we build things on earth in the same way?

The value of the gold and silver does not take into account the total cost of materials and labor to construct. The Temple of Solomon was hand made and assembled on site without the sound of a saw or a hammer.

In distress David gathered the gold, silver and materials for the Temple by the thousands. Many people think that they will be able to give to the Lord when things settle down. It doesn't work that way. You will learn that prosperity comes out of pressure and pain, not after them.

1 Chronicles 29:2-4

Now I have prepared with all my might for the house of my God the gold for *things to be made* of gold, and the silver for *things* of silver, and the brass for *things* of brass, the iron for *things* of iron, and wood for *things* of wood; onyx stones, and *stones* to be set, glistering stones, and of divers colors, and all manner of precious stones, and marble stones in abundance. [3]More over, because I have set my affection to the house of my God, I have of mine own proper good, of gold and silver, *which* I have given to the house of my God, over and above all that I have prepared for the holy house, [4]*Even* three **thousand** talents of gold, of the gold of Ophir, and seven **thousand** talents of refined silver, to overlay the walls of the houses:

David not only secured the 100,000 talents of gold from the nation for the Temple, he gave 3000 talents of gold from his own personal reserve, plus many other costly items. David was a very wealthy king indeed, whose heart was purposed to build kingdom things. David obtained his wealth by defeating his enemies in battle through the Spirit of the Lord.

Solomon did not have to fight with enemies because his father David defeated all of them. God has done the same thing for you. You do not have to fight to obtain prosperity because Jesus has won that battle for you. The only battle you are to engage in is the good fight of faith that will produce prosperity and all of the promises of God for you.

Solomon only knew peace but he benefited from the price that his father David paid. We should reap the rewards of the spoils that Jesus took from the devil at Calvary and return them back into the Kingdom of God where they belong. David did this for the nation of Israel and for the Kingdom of God. When

David defeated the city of Rabbah he took the city and destroyed the Ammonites in it. David then spoiled them of all of their possessions, including the crown of the King of the Ammonites.

1 Chronicles 20:2
And David took the crown of their king from off his head, and found it to weigh a talent of gold, and *there were* precious stones in it; and it was set upon David's head: and he brought also exceeding much spoil out of the city.

The crown of gold weighed one talent. Again a talent is equal to approximately 94 pounds. This crown was made from solid gold. You would have to agree that the gold of a king's crown would probably be the best gold available. So based on the formula used for the Platinum American Eagle Gold comparison, the crown on David's head would look like this in our current dollar standard:

1 talent x 94 pounds x 16 ounces = 1,504 total ounces of gold

1,504 ounces x $1,840.30 = $2,767,811.20

David's gold crown on the market today would be worth nearly 3 million dollars. That is only the value of the gold itself.

The gold has a measureable value, it is symbolic of the fact that God wants us to know that there is a portion of prosperity for every believer. 94 pounds is a lot of weight to place on your head. This tells us something about David.

David was well able to support the weight of the prosperity upon his head. One, he had a strong neck, not a stiff one. A stiff neck won't turn when God speaks; a strong neck can. He emblematically shows us that God's people are able to carry prosperity in their life and that every person in the royal family of God can handle as much as 3 million dollars without getting off course or losing their balance.

This does not include the value of the precious stones inlaid in the crown. We can estimate the monetary value of the gold because of the finite weight. But how can you measure the infinite value of the precious stones inlaid in it?

We do not even know what kind of stones they were. Even if we knew the type and number of stones inlaid in the crown, we would have a tough time figuring the value of the stones. All precious gems are not created equal. The price of the stones depends on their cut, clarity and color. Each gem has an individual appraisal. The stones inlaid in the crown represent the individual rewards for every believer. Your appraisal is directly proportionate to your rewards.

The precious stones represent the equity of our lives that cannot be measured numerically. People may not see your true value on the surface, but that does not change God's value of you. There is much to be said about the subject of crowns and I will leave that for another time, but you should know this: David took the crown from the enemy king just as Jesus took the spoils from the devil and triumphed over him in it.

The jewels in the crown are the anointing and blessing of God that cannot be compared to mere money; they are symbolic of the true riches of the anointing of God. When you operate with the level of wealth that David and Solomon did, money will be the last thing on your mind. Money should be the last thing on your mind because you should have such an abundance of money to complete your assignments that you don't have to contend with finding the money to sustain your cause.

Solomon did not have to think about money a single day of his life. His father gave him plenty of wealth and riches and God multiplied it a thousandfold. God made Solomon extremely rich and wealthy. God said that there would not be a king as rich as he would be either before him or after him. Essentially God was backdating Solomon's prosperity.

Endorsing a document by a date earlier than the one on which the document was originally drawn up is backdating. Under most circumstances, backdating is seen as fraudulent and illegal, although there are some situations in which backdating can be used in a legal and beneficial way, such as backdating a claim for a past period.

Sometimes certain claims (such as insurance claims) can be backdated if they could not be completed at an earlier date, although there must be good reason for neglecting to claim in advance. If your backdated claim is approved, you will be able to receive benefits from a certain date in the past like back wages and benefits.

God essentially told Solomon that He was backdating his prosperity by telling him that his prosperity would be larger than anyone before or after him.

1 Kings 3:12-13

Behold, I have done according to your words: lo, I have given you a wise and an understanding heart; so that there was none like you before you, neither after you shall any arise like unto you. [13]And I have also given you that which you have not asked, both riches, and honor: so that there shall not be any among the kings like unto you all your days.

The thousandfold principle is an eternal principle. Eternity goes as far back as it goes forward. This is because eternity exists outside the realm of time. Thousandfold prosperity can enable you to reach back in time by faith and lay claim on the things that may have been misplaced or stolen. God has restored your financial position now you must use your faith and the thousandfold principle of seedtime and harvest to lay hold on them. The Bible gives details of some of the wealth that came to Solomon because of the wisdom of God in him.

2 Chronicles 9:23-25
And all the kings of the earth sought the presence of Solomon, to hear his wisdom, that God had put in his heart. [24]And they brought every man his present, vessels of silver, and vessels of gold, and raiment, harness, and spices, horses, and mules, a rate year by year. [25]And Solomon had four thousand stalls for horses and chariots, and twelve thousand horsemen; whom he bestowed in the chariot cities, and with the king at Jerusalem.

2 Chronicles 9:13-14
Now the weight of gold that came to Solomon in one year was six hundred and threescore and six talents of gold; [14]Beside *that which* chapmen and merchants brought. And all the kings of Arabia and governors of the country brought gold and silver to Solomon.

Solomon received 666 talents of gold each year plus the gold and silver that came to him from trading and business deals. Every year for forty years Solomon's personal salary may have exceeded as much as three billion dollars per year. The king was tax exempt while on the throne, so Solomon's earned income during his career was in excess of 120 billion dollars.

You may think that this level of income is just for Bible kings or exclusive to Solomon, but it is not. Religion and tradition has squashed the finances of covenant people into thinking that there is barely enough to go around and that it is arrogant and selfish to have more money than you need to get by. This is the theme of the anti-prosperity puppeteers that cast dispersions on people at large keeping them from taking hold of the thousandfold lifestyle.

Everything in the Kingdom of God is built on the foundation of the thousandfold system. All of the materials, laborers, priests, musicians, judges and officers involved in the temple project were all numbered by the thousands.

1 Chronicles 23:1-5

So when David was old and full of days, he made Solomon his son king over Israel. [2]And he gathered together all the princes of Israel, with the priests and the Levites. [3]Now the Levites were numbered from the age of thirty years and upward: and their number by their polls, man by man, was thirty and eight thousand. [4]Of which, twenty and four thousand *were* to set forward the work of the house of the LORD; and six thousand *were* officers and judges: [5]Moreover four thousand *were* porters; and four thousand praised the LORD with the instruments which I made, *said David*, to praise *therewith*.

The Temple of Solomon was built, supervised and manned by workers that were numbered by the thousands. Thousandfold people built the Temple of Solomon.

God does everything by the measure. The great thing about the measure system is that it allows everyone to participate in the Kingdom blessing of giving and receiving equitably. It doesn't matter if you have much or little, when you give and receive by the measure, the Kingdom principles of prosperity and blessing work for you. So if a widow gives all she has and a king gives a bigger portion from his abundance, God will activate the thousandfold blessing for both parties.

God knows the exact amount of money you give to Him but he blesses you by its measure. If you are rich, giving a lot of money may not mean you have given a thousandfold measure. Whereas giving a large measure of a little money can. Jesus said that the widow's two mites in Mark Chapter 12 outranked the entire offering of all of the rich put together.

I am not advocating that we are competing for a financial prize. I am saying that the thousandfold principle is completely fair because it allows anyone to participate no matter how much money they have to give. God is pleased for you to prosper and He has empowered you to obtain wealth and riches for the purpose of advancing the Kingdom of God. Preaching the whole Gospel includes teaching the word of God and should be followed by signs and wonders confirming the word of God. The Gospel has been fully preached when all of the nations are blessed with the promise that God gave to Abraham.

This means that the people hear the word of God and we as the church are financially able to feed the hungry, clothe the naked and visit the sick and imprisoned. After all, we will all be judged not for our sins but for what we did for those who are less fortunate than us. Every Christian should want to prosper for the purpose of being a blessing to others. You may not think that you are supposed to walk in the thousandfold blessing, but consider the following facts from globalissues.org that should encourage you to become thousandfold prosperous:

- One third of the world's population has never owned a pair of shoes.
- Two thirds of the world makes less than a dollar a day.
- Half of the world eats rice as their only staple.
- 22,000 children a day die from starvation and disease.
- 1 billion people cannot read or write.
- 40 million people live with HIV/Aids
- 1.1 billion people have no access to clean drinking water.
- 1.8 million children die each year from diarrhea.
- Half of the 2.2 billion children in the world live in poverty.
- 10.6 million children died before the age of 5 in 2003.
- 15 million children are orphaned.
- 2.5 billion people depend on wood, charcoal or animal dung for energy.

There is a huge gap between the have's and the have not's. According to the report from globalissues.org there are 497 billionaires out of 6.7 billion people on planet earth. There are approximately 10 million millionaires around the world. These two groups of rich and wealthy people control the lion's share of the wealth. These affluent people are also the people who form and shape policy that dictates the way we live.

The people of God should be those who are the shakers and movers in society. Recently 40 of the world's billionaires decided to come into agreement to give half of their wealth to the poor and needy around the world. This is among a group of people that do not necessarily proclaim Jesus as their Lord and

Savior. They may not know Christ but they are acting on the principles that meet with the approval of the Heavenly Father.

What would you do if you could get up in the morning and not think about money as a means of getting by but rather as a means of saving lives? What if money was the last thing on your mind? How would that change the way you live? The answer to these questions is discovered in the way you handle money now. Remember, faithful in the least is faithful in the much.

God blesses us to be a blessing. The thousandfold principle empowers you to become rich and wealthy for the purpose of helping others. Thousandfold prosperity will empower you to be the one who can make the difference for the children, the poor and destitute in this world. You can be the person who stands in the widening gap between life and death for millions around the world.

Chapter 10
Thousandfold Anointing

Life goes on after this age is completed. After the resurrection of the dead in Christ and the rapture of those who are alive and remain, God has plans to create a new heaven and a new earth for us to reign and rule with Him. We will continue to function and operate on the New Earth much the same as we do now, but without sin, curse or the devil. We will carry on the tasks and functions we did in this life the way God originally intended, but for eternity.

On this side of Heaven we learn to apply our faith in the principles of the word of God in pursuit of perfection. Like all of the principles in the word of God, the thousandfold principle will operate forever. In this world you are learning how to function in the kingdom of God through kingdom principles so that you can become a more proficient believer now and forever.

The time you invest now in the Kingdom of God will qualify you for the eternal ages to come. That is why it is so important to be faithful over the things that God has given to you. They may seem small and insignificant at first, but God watches over your stewardship and rewards you accordingly. We all must be accountable for the way we handled the things God assigned for us to accomplish. When you are faithful in the smaller things it proves that you can be trusted with the greater things.

Faith is distinct from faithfulness. Faith is the substance of things hoped for and the evidence of things not seen. It is the tangible proof of the things that we believe in God's word. Faith establishes the existence of all things. Faithfulness means to do the best you can with what you have or to be trustworthy. Faith is a noun but faithfulness is a verb. Some people have the responsibility over a household while others have the responsibility over a corporation. Faithfulness over either one will cause abundance to flow into your life.

Proverbs 28:20
A faithful man shall abound with blessings: but he that makes haste to be rich shall not be innocent.

A person who does the very best they can with what they have is considered faithful. A faithful person is certain, trustworthy and reliable. They can watch over other people's possessions and treasures without concern for loss or theft. They are known for their integrity and ability to bring a profitable return. True faithfulness is not measured by how you handle your own wealth, true faithfulness is measured by the way you handle another person's wealth.

Luke 16:10-12
He that is faithful in that which is least is faithful also in much: and he that is unjust in the least is unjust also in much. [11]If therefore you have not been faithful in the unrighteous mammon, who will commit to your trust the true *riches*? [12]And if you have not been faithful in that which is another persons, who shall give you that which is your own?

Jesus said that the reward for faithfulness was true riches. True riches is the highest level of riches attainable. The way you handle other types of riches determines the measure God can trust you with. There are three different types of riches listed in the word of God.

Uncertain Riches

1 Timothy 6:17

Charge them that are rich in this world, that they be not high minded, nor trust in uncertain riches, but in the living God, who gives us richly all things to enjoy;

Uncertain riches is the money kept on the earth and subject to loss. Jesus said to lay up treasures in heaven so that the elements and thieves of the earth do not destroy them, like recession, inflation and taxes.

Durable Riches

Proverbs 8:17-18

I love them that love me; and those that seek me early shall find me. [18]Riches and honor *are* with me; *yea*, durable riches and righteousness.

Durable riches comes from wisdom. Durable in the Hebrew text means antique or valued riches. Long lasting substance is the product of wisdom and honor. This is the thousandfold wealth in the natural realm for the believer.

True Riches

Luke 16:11

If therefore you have not been faithful in the unrighteous mammon, who will commit to your trust the true *riches*?

True riches is a product of the anointing of God that releases the miracle dunamis power of God. You cannot buy the anointing or power of God but you do have to prove yourself faithful. The way that God proves faithfulness in you is through the fashion in which you handle another entity's wealth. If you can be trusted to carry someone else's money then you can be trusted to carry your own.

Luke 16:12
And if ye have not been faithful in that which is another man's, who shall give you that which is your own?

The anointing is the ability of God to remove burdens and destroy yokes of bondage. It is God's resident power to dissolve symptoms and obliterate sources of sickness, disease, poverty and destruction. The anointing is the most valuable commodity in existence. Your parents generally will not hand over the keys to a new automobile if you are not first proven faithful over the family car. God will not release the true riches of the anointing upon you if you are not first proven faithful in all things, including money.

You must first be qualified before you can be multiplied. This includes your personal money, the money you handle for the company you work for and God's money including the tithes and the offerings. Stewardship is related to faithfulness.

1 Corinthians 4:2
Moreover it is required in stewards, that you be found faithful.
Amplified
Moreover, it is [essentially] required of stewards that a man should be found faithful [proving himself worthy of trust].

Faithfulness is the currency of the anointing. The gift of salvation is free but you will have to pay a price for the things of the Kingdom of God. The anointing is dealt out in measure to you according to your stewardship. The more faithful you are, the more anointing you can carry. God does not arbitrarily pour His anointing upon your life. He issues the amount of anointing in your life in direct relation to the faithfulness you show to Him.

There is no lack of anointing. The believer that is proven and qualified will carry as much anointing as they have qualified themselves for through their financial stewardship. One of the reasons that you do not see as many miracles today, as there have been in the past, is because the financial stewardship of the Church is a mess. Most do not tithe to God and many give nothing at all in the Kingdom.

The main cause of this condition is greed. It is more satisfying to the flesh to hold onto the money you have than to sow it. That is why so many latch onto the lies of the devil. You will never know the true riches if you adapt to this demonic thinking.

I have established that there is a direct connection between stewardship and the anointing. In Luke 16 Jesus addressed faithfulness and true riches. He further explains that if we master money then money will not master us.

Luke 16:13
No servant can serve two masters: for either he will hate the one, and love the other; or else he will hold to the one, and despise the other. You cannot serve God and mammon.

181

Mammon is a transliteration of an Aramaic word that means wealth, riches or earthly goods. Mammon amounts to materialism. In that day Mammon was the name of a Syrian money god, Strong's #3126 defines it as, confidence in material wealth personified. It is an avarice or extreme greed for wealth.

When you are not faithful with another party's wealth and riches then you are disqualified for larger portions of wealth and riches. Holding back money is stealing. That's why Malachi 3:8 asks the question, "Will a person rob God?" When you rob God you are robbing yourself. You are robbing God of what rightfully belongs to him and you rob yourself of the opportunity to be blessed. When you keep back or abuse the privilege of handling someone else's wealth, you are demonstrating that you are overtaken by greed. Jesus did not say that you shouldn't have money, what He said was money shouldn't have you.

If you are greedy, you serve money as a personified god. Money becomes more than a neutral tool to exchange things with, it becomes the false god that you will bow down and worship. This will cause you to transgress and sin against the true God of Heaven. The anointing of God will not flow in the measure you need until you are reconciled financially with God's economic system.

You were not designed to serve money because money was designed to serve you. The word serve comes from the Greek word that means to be in bondage to as a slave. You do not want to be a slave to money. When you are a slave to money it dictates how you live your life. God does not want you to have to worry about money. Money should be the last thing on your mind.

Jesus said that you couldn't serve two masters. Your heart cannot be divided between God and money. You can only follow after one master. God has to be first in your life before you can master money.

Matthew 6:33
But seek you first the kingdom of God, and his righteousness; and all these things shall be added unto you.

When you are in right standing with God financially, then your thinking about money will change and then money will begin to flow through your life the way God intended it to, in thousandfold measure. When you seek after God then money will seek after you. The word seek in the Greek is the word that means to worship and desire. You will worship, seek and desire whatever you love. If you love God you will not fall into the snare and deceitfulness of riches, but if you love money it will become a trap to you.

You are supposed to be money's master not its slave. You will only master money when you understand its real purpose. According to King Solomon, money answers all things; however, money is powerless to change anything by itself. It takes the anointing to make real change in this world.

It is often misquoted that money is the root of all evil. Money is neither good nor bad, money is neutral. Money is not inherently evil. If money was inherently evil then satan would try to get as much of it in your life as he could. The motivation behind the usage of money can be good or bad but money itself is not evil. Money is not the basis of all evil, it is the love of money that is the basis of all wickedness in this world.

183

1 Timothy 6:10

For the love of money is the root of all evil: which while some coveted after, they have erred from the faith, and pierced themselves through with many sorrows.

You do not have to have a lot of money to love it. Greed fuels both the rich and poor alike. When God is your master, money will be your servant. Everybody needs a constant flow of money in order to live but until you have a consistent lifestyle of praise and worship to God, then you will not have a consistent flow of money either.

Most people do not fully understand the purpose of money. If you do not understand the purpose of something then you will tend to abuse it. Money is used for the exchange of goods and services. Money is generally printed on paper currency in the form of promissory notes. The promissory notes represent the value of the gold behind it.

We use paper and electronic banking to process money transactions. Paper money represents the amount of gold that a federal reserve of a country will back it with. Up until the 1930's, people could take money to the bank and exchange it for the same amount of dollars in gold coins. The Constitution of the United States actually required that money be produced in metal and not in paper. This was designed to prevent the government from circulating more money than they had gold to back it with.

Inflation can happen when governments print an excess of money to deal with a crisis. As a result, prices end up rising at an extremely high speed to keep up with the currency surplus.

This is called the demand-pull, in which prices are forced upwards because of a high demand.

So what is so important about gold? Why is gold used as the standard for money? Gold is one of three of the most rare precious metals in the earth including platinum and silver. Gold is impervious to the elements and will maintain its composition indefinitely. Gold can transfer electricity with less resistance than any other metal. Extremely high-end electronics and computer components use gold wiring instead of copper for their circuitry. Gold does not corrode and it is used to plate or make fine electrical contacts. Gold is the standard that God chose for wealth and riches in Heaven and on the earth.

In Heaven God uses gold to pave streets and build entire cities. Gold is the primary supply of building materials for the infrastructure in Heaven. Gold is thousandfold in endless supply in Heaven. On the earth there is not near as much gold in circulation as there will be. The total amount of gold mined to date would fit in a 150' square cube. That does not mean that there is a lack of gold in the earth. Gold is a rare commodity but it is not in short supply, we just have not located the abundant supply God placed in the planet yet.

Psalm 104:24
O LORD, how manifold are your works! in wisdom have you made them all: the earth is full of your riches.

God created the heaven and the earth and He placed all of the provisions in the earth that man would need forever. The earth is full of God's riches including gold. I like to say that the earth is God's wallet. Most of the gold mined today comes from

185

South Africa. The United States has the largest gold reserve in the modern world.

God's original plan for gold was not to use it as a means for buying and selling goods and services. God's original purpose for gold is the same purpose that He uses it for in Heaven, which is to build things. God not only uses gold for construction materials, He uses many other precious gems as well. Throughout the Bible there are numerous examples of this truth. From the Tabernacle to the Temple, gold was used as a primary material for building.

Revelation 21:18-21

And the building of the wall of it was *of* jasper: and the city *was* pure gold, like unto clear glass. [19]And the foundations of the wall of the city *were* garnished with all manner of precious stones. The first foundation *was* jasper; the second, sapphire; the third, a chalcedony; the fourth, an emerald; [20]The fifth, sardonyx; the sixth, sardius; the seventh, chrysolite; the eighth, beryl; the ninth, a topaz; the tenth, a chrysoprasus; the eleventh, a jacinth; the twelfth, an amethyst. [21]And the twelve gates *were* twelve pearls; every several gate was of one pearl: and the street of the city *was* pure gold, as it were transparent glass.

If you went shopping at the building supply store in Heaven, you would not look for the concrete and drywall aisles. You would look for the gold, silver and precious gems isles. The idea of using precious metals and stones to build things is not reserved for Heaven alone.

The Temple of Solomon is a perfect example of how the gold was used for construction. Many tons of gold was used to build the Temple of Solomon. God never intended for mankind to use gold as money. God originally placed gold in the Garden of Eden as a source for manufacturing and fabrication of buildings and infrastructure.

Genesis 2:10-14
And a river went out of Eden to water the garden; and from thence it was parted, and became into four heads. [11]The name of the first is Pison: that is it which compasses the whole land of Havilah, where there is gold; [12]And the gold of that land is good: there is bdellium and the onyx stone. [13]And the name of the second river is Gihon: the same is it that compasses the whole land of Ethiopia. [14]And the name of the third river is Hiddekel: that is it which goes toward the east of Assyria. And the fourth river is Euphrates.

The word for river in the Hebrew is Na-hawr, which means prosperity. The river of God flowed into the earth and proceeded from Eden to water the garden. The river of God branched into four separate heads and carried supplies to the Garden of Eden. All four of the rivers have a specific meaning that pertains to increase and advancement.

River of God: Prosperity

- Pison: Dispersive, Spread Out
- Gihon: Gush Forth
- Hiddekel: Rapid
- Euphrates: Break Forth

The Hiddekel and Euphrates rivers still appear in the post Noah maps. The other two rivers' locations are not known. These two rivers were likely displaced after Noah's flood, their location today is speculative. The interesting thing about this

187

original river system is that it functions opposite to rivers as we know them. Most rivers are fed by tributaries and then become one stream from those bodies of water. The Garden of Eden describes a single river splitting into four individual streams.

The original river came from Heaven and then flowed into the earth through the Garden of Eden.

Psalm 46:4-5

There is a river, the streams whereof shall make glad **the city of God**, the holy *place* of the tabernacles of the most High. [5]God *is* in the midst of her; she shall not be moved: God shall help her, *and that* right early.

Psalm 65:9-10

You visit the earth, and water it: you greatly enrich it with **the river of God,** *which* is full of water: you prepare them corn, when you have so provided for it. [10]You water the ridges thereof abundantly: you settles the furrows thereof: you make it soft with showers: you bless the springing thereof.

The River of God is connected to the river in Revelation Chapter 22, which flows through the middle of a street made out of solid gold. That river feeds the four rivers in Genesis Chapter 2.

Revelation 22:1-2

And he showed me a **pure river of water of life**, clear as crystal, proceeding out of the throne of God and of the Lamb. [2]In the midst of the street of it, and on either side of the river, *was there* the tree of life, which bare twelve *manner of* fruits, *and* yielded her fruit every month: and the leaves of the tree *were* for the healing of the nations.

The first river is the Pison River and it is described as surrounding the land of Havilah. Havilah means circular. The Pison River flowed in a circle. The circle speaks of eternity. I know it does not make sense for a river to move in circular motion but we are not looking at this from a natural standpoint.

The River of God not only flows through the street of gold in Heaven, it proceeds from the Lamb of God and the throne He sits upon. The River of God comes out of the belly, or Spirit of God. This is the flow of the Holy Spirit into the earth to produce the blessing of God for all mankind. It is what connected Heaven and Earth before the curse of sin broke out and disrupted the flow, and it is what is re-connected after the outpouring of the Holy Spirit.

The River of God feeds the four rivers in Eden with an aggressive and powerful force of current that disperses and breaks through into your life. Therefore we can see how the river system of the Garden of Eden gave mankind natural supply and spiritual supply. There are three things that the believer can draw from the currents of the rivers:

Prosperity
Psalm 1:3
And they shall be like a tree planted by the rivers of water, that brings forth their fruit in season; their leaf also shall not wither; and whatsoever they doeth shall prosper.

Presence
Isaiah 33:21
But there the glorious LORD *will be* unto us a place of broad rivers *and* streams; wherein shall go no galley with oars, neither shall gallant ship pass thereby.

Living Bible

The glorious Lord will be to us as a wide river of protection, and no enemy can cross.

Peace

Isaiah 66:12

For thus says the LORD, Behold, I will extend peace to her like a river, and the glory of the Gentiles like a flowing stream: then shall you suck, you shall be borne upon *her* sides, and be dandled upon *her* knees.

The multiple rivers of God contain the life and promise of God's word and His Kingdom for you. Jesus said that the Holy Spirit would cause multiple rivers to spring forth from our life.

John 7:38-39

He that believeth on me, as the scripture has said, out of his belly shall flow rivers of living water. [39](But this spoke he of the Spirit, which they that believe on him should receive: for the Holy Ghost was not yet *given*; because that Jesus was not yet glorified.)

The rivers of the Spirit will flow from within your heart and life when you invite the Holy Spirit to dwell in your life. These rivers will spring forth from your life to create multiple streams of wealth and riches.

There is a parallel image in the Garden of Eden that every believer should take hold of. The four rivers that proceed from the River of God are a picture of the multi-stream blessing of God. Many people depend on one income to live on. If that income stops, their life stops. If you have more than one income then you will be sustained financially.

The Israelites were told to tithe from four different sources of income.

Deuteronomy 14:22-23

You shall truly tithe all the increase of your seed, that the field brings forth year by year. [23]And you shall eat before the LORD your God, in the place which he shall choose to place His name there, the tithe of your **corn**, of your **wine**, and of your **oil**, and the firstlings of your **herds and of your flocks**; that you may learn to fear the LORD your God always.

They had four streams of income to live on and give from. God wants you to tap into the thousandfold river and flow with the four fold streams from your life. If you have four streams of income then you will never know lack. If one stream is not producing as much as usual then the other streams make up the difference. Every believer should have at least four sources of revenue.

God does not want you to lack any good thing, and money is a good thing. The thousandfold wisdom of God will produce witty ideas to prosper for the Kingdom of God and the preaching of the Gospel to the world. The Church needs much more money than it presently has so that we can complete the assignment of the Great Commission, and preach the gospel of the Kingdom of God to every nation and the end to come.

God wants to prosper you with the unlimited thousandfold power and purpose of His Holy Spirit and anointing. The thousandfold anointing will release unlimited miracles, signs and wonders that will win the lost and defeat satan. When you apply the principles of seedtime and harvest through giving and receiving in the Kingdom of Heaven, God will loose boundless dunamis power as a witness of God's goodness, grace and glory.

There is a direct connection between money and the anointing. Whenever gold was brought to the House of God, His glory and power showed up. This occurred in the building of the Tabernacle of Moses and the building of the Temple of Solomon.

1 Kings 8:10-11

And it came to pass, when the priests were come out of the holy *place*, that the cloud filled the house of the LORD, [11]So that the priests could not stand to minister because of the cloud: for the glory of the LORD had filled the house of the LORD.

When the gold returns to the house of God, then the glory will fill the house. The gold always precedes the glory. Both the Tabernacle of Moses and the Temple of Solomon used gold in their construction. In the Tabernacle of Moses the gold came from the spoils of the Egyptians after Israel was delivered from slavery. The gold in the Temple of Solomon came through the spoils of war that David fought and by the gifts that came to Solomon from foreign nations. In both cases there was transference of the wealth from the wicked nations to the just nation of Israel.

God's word promises that the wealth of the wicked is laid up in store for the just. The body of Christ is the just it is reserved for. There will be a significant end time wealth transfer from the wicked to the Church in this last day. God stakes His claim on all of the silver and all of the gold, and He will cause it to migrate back to His house so that the latter day glory will appear over the house of God.

Haggai 2:6-9

For thus says the LORD of hosts; Yet once, it *is* a little while, and I will shake the heavens, and the earth, and the sea, and the dry *land*; [7]And I will shake all nations, and the desire of all nations shall come: and I will fill this house with glory, says the LORD of hosts. [8]The silver *is* mine, and the gold *is* mine, says the LORD of hosts. [9]The glory of this latter house shall be greater than of the former, says the LORD of hosts: and in this place will I give peace, says the LORD of hosts.

All of the material wealth in the world belongs to God. Haggai prophesied concerning the restoration of the Temple, known as Zerubbabel's Temple. This is the temple that was built when Israel returned from the captivity in Babylon.

Zerubbabel, a direct descendant of King David, became the Governor over Israel. He was commissioned to build the house of God in the place where the Temple of Solomon was originally built. It took nearly 21 years to finish the Temple from the time Israel left Babylon. When the Temple was completed, he restored the vessels used for worship in the Temple of Solomon that were taken by Nebuchadnezzar, the King of Babylon.

Zerubbabel went through political opposition and national indifference but he prevailed to complete the project. The prophets Haggai and Zechariah were both instrumental in the process. God used these two prophets to speak prophetically to encourage Zerubbabel. Haggai's prophecy explained why the nation of Israel was enduring financial hardship and what they needed to do to turn it around.

Haggai 1:5-8

Now therefore thus says the LORD of hosts; Consider your ways. [6]You have sown much, and bring in little; you eat, but you have not enough; you drink, but you are not filled with drink; you clothe you, but there is none warm; and he that earns wages earns wages *to put it* into a bag with holes. [7]Thus says the LORD of hosts; Consider your ways. [8]Go up to the mountain, and bring wood, and build the house; and I will take pleasure in it, and I will be glorified, says the LORD.

God's glory always follows when the gold and silver is returned to the Lord to build His house. Israel received this word from Haggai after they had left the captivity of Babylon. God told them that after seventy years were accomplished that the people would return to the promise land of their fathers. A heathen King named Cyrus of Persia overthrew the Babylonians and sent the people of God back to their homeland. God anointed Cyrus to accomplish this and He used the prophet Isaiah to speak this word to the captives while they were in Babylon.

When Cyrus released the people of God back to their homeland, he sent them with silver and gold and the Persian citizens gave the Israelites gifts too. Unfortunately, Israel forgot the word of the Lord, they focused on building their own houses and they neglected the building of the Temple to restore worship back to the nation.

Haggai admonished the people to return to the building of the Temple and in so doing they would turn the economy around in their favor. I believe that is why the economy is struggling today. The Church has forgotten to put the building of the Kingdom of God first and they have withheld the gold and silver that belongs in the Kingdom.

The Lord said that He would shake the nations and the desire of the nations would come to the Temple. The word desire is the Hebrew word for treasure. God said that the latter house would be greater in glory than the former house. That means God will cause a financial movement by His Spirit to move gold and silver into the hands of God's people for the purpose of building His house. God's house is the Temple of the Holy Spirit. The Apostle Paul said that Christians are the Temple of the Holy Spirit.

Previously I stated that the purpose of gold and silver was for building materials. The Temple of Solomon was build out of literal gold, silver and other precious jewels. The Spiritual Temple of the believer is built through gold and silver as well. Gold and silver produce the means to preach the Gospel to the nations. The Gospel saves the lost and converts them into the children of God. So here we can see that the real purpose of gold and silver is to win souls and build lives.

When gold and silver are used for their true purpose, then the power principle of the thousandfold anointing will be released and the Gospel will be fully preached to the nations of the world, bringing this age to a close. The glory of God follows the return of the gold to the House of God. The anointing of God follows the giving of money to the Lord. The unlimited thousandfold power of God is then released on the people.

On the Day of Penetecost, the Holy Spirit was poured out upon all of the people who received Him. The outpouring of God's Holy Spirit on all flesh was the promise of the Father spoken by the prophet Joel. This promise brought the fulfillment of the presence of the anointing of God on anyone who receives Him.

The Apostles preached the word with power and authority and thousands got saved from their messages. The New Testament Church began to grow daily and the people responded with their giving.

Acts 2:44-47

And all that believed were together, and had all things common; [45]And sold their possessions and goods, and parted them to all *men*, as every man had need. [46]And they, continuing daily with one accord in the temple, and breaking bread from house to house, did eat their meat with gladness and singleness of heart, [47]Praising God, and having favor with all the people. And the Lord added to the church daily such as should be saved.

The anointing of God caused the believers to come together and bring their wealth together as one. Nobody in the Church had any needs. One of the effects of the anointing was complete debt cancelation and ample supply of provisions.

Acts 4:32-35

And the multitude of them that believed were of one heart and of one soul: neither said any *of them* that ought of the things which he possessed was his own; but they had all things common. [33]And with great power gave the apostles witness of the resurrection of the Lord Jesus: and great grace was upon them all. [34]Neither was there any among them that lacked: for as many as were possessors of lands or houses sold them, and brought the prices of the things that were sold, [35]And laid *them* down at the apostles' feet: and distribution was made unto every man according as he had need.

The newborn church thought alike, believed alike and acted alike. The Holy Spirit brought unity to the believers and their wealth. They sold their possessions and gave the entire amount to take care of all of the needs of the body of Christ. Whenever you give like this the thousandfold principle kicks in. Notice that as a result of the people's generosity, the power and anointing of the Holy Spirit came forth as a witness of the resurrection power of Jesus Christ.

The thousandfold principle releases the unlimited blessing and empowerment of God's Kingdom. Great grace and great power flow as evidence of God's glory and anointing. Today the church should have more power and favor than the early church had. Haggai said the glory of the latter house would be greater than the glory of the former house. The thousandfold anointing of God will bring about the manifest glory of God in proportion to the gifts that come into the Kingdom of God.

Your thousandfold gift will accomplish the same things for you. Expect God to move upon your life with dunamis power and great favor. When the Body of Christ takes hold of this message and works together as a corporate body of believers, God will release His thousandfold anointing.

Chapter 11
Thousandfold Generation

The thousandfold principle is an eternal principle that will be used for end time events. The world as we know it is scheduled to end. There is a difference between the world and the earth. The earth is the planet that God created for the benefit and pleasure of mankind. The world is the social political system that functions on the earth. God is the God of the whole earth.

Isaiah 54:5
For your Maker *is* thine husband; the LORD of hosts *is* his name; and your Redeemer the Holy One of Israel; The God of the whole earth shall he be called.

The Greek word for world is kosmos, which is where we get the word cosmopolitan or worldly. The Bible says that satan is the god of this world. He is not the god of the earth. The devil is the god of the kosmos. The devil rules over the political social realm of fallen man.

2 Corinthians 4:4
In whom the god of this world has blinded the minds of them, which believe not, lest the light of the glorious gospel of Christ, who is the image of God, should shine unto them.

The devil never had control or rights to the earth. The ownership of the earth belongs to God.

Psalm 24:1-2

The earth *is* the LORD'S, and the fullness thereof; the world, and they that dwell therein. ^{2}For he has founded it upon the seas, and established it upon the floods.

When you buy property or land there will be a deed drawn up giving your name as registered owner of the property. Psalm 24:1 is the verse that makes the statement of the title deed for planet earth. God made all things in creation. Planet Earth belongs to God. Earth was created by the spoken word of God and the earth was built for habitation by human beings forever.

Sin and the curse that came upon man and the planet shortened the plan for the earth to last for eternity. God made the planet and everything that is on it for the benefit and advantage of mankind. God then gave the earth to mankind so we could reign and rule over it the way God rules over the heaven.

Psalm 115:15-16

You *are* blessed of the LORD, which made heaven and earth. ^{16}The heaven, *even* the heavens, *are* the LORD'S: but the earth hath he given to the children of men.

Contrary to popular belief, God gave the control of the earth to man. Many Christians mistakenly think that God is in control over what happens in the world. The phrase "God is in control" is often repeated when people really don't understand what to do. God is sovereign and He is the Lord of all things. However, when God gave Adam the command to dress and keep the Garden of Eden, He was handing the keys of the domain of the earth over to Adam male and female. God can intervene in your affairs if you invite Him to as long as you allow him access through your will and faith in Him. Some people take issue with me over this point because they are ignorant of the word of God. They simply cannot accept the fact that God placed man in a position just below Himself even though the scriptures support that position.

Psalm 8:3-9

When I consider your heavens, the work of your fingers, the moon and the stars, which you have ordained; [4]What is man, that you are mindful of him? and the son of man, that you visits him? [5]For you have made him a little lower than the angels, and have crowned him with glory and honor. [6]You made him to have dominion over the works of your hands; you have put all *things* under his feet: [7]All sheep and oxen, yes, and the beasts of the field; [8]The fowl of the air, and the fish of the sea, *and whatsoever* passes through the paths of the seas. [9]O LORD our Lord, how excellent *is* your name in all the earth!

God gave mankind the dominion and authority over everything that moved on the earth including everything that swims, flies or crawls on the planet. Nothing on the planet could move unless it passed through Adam first.

God made man in His image and in His likeness. That means you are made with God-given ability and God-given appearance. The first commandment that God gave to Adam was to increase by fruitfulness and multiplication.

Genesis 1:27-28

So God created man in his *own* image, in the image of God created he him; male and female created he them. [28]And God blessed them, and God said unto them, Be fruitful, and multiply, and replenish the earth, and subdue it: and have dominion over

201

the fish of the sea, and over the fowl of the air, and over every living thing that moves upon the earth.

The authority of the entire planet was originally given to mankind. God made man to have dominion and authority over the works of His hands. Adam was given the same miracle working power that God used to create the heavens and the earth. The reason many stumble over the fact that man is made a little lower than God Himself is due to the incorrect translation. The word angels is the Hebrew word Elohim, which is the word for gods. The correct rendering is that man was made a little lower than God. The New Testament writer in the book of Hebrews quotes this same passage in Psalms Chapter 8 the same way it reads in the Old Testament.

Hebrews 2:5-9

For unto the angels has he not put in subjection the world to come, whereof we speak. [6]But one in a certain place testified, saying, What is man, that you are mindful of him? or the son of man, that you visits him? [7]You made him a little lower than the angels; you crown him with glory and honor, and did set him over the works of your hands: [8]You have put all things in subjection under his feet. For in that he put all in subjection under him, he left nothing *that is* not put under him. But now we see not yet all things put under him. [9]But we see Jesus, who was made a little lower than the angels for the suffering of death, crowned with glory and honor; that he by the grace of God should taste death for every man.

The writer of Hebrews copied the text from Psalm Chapter 8 verbatim. The New Testament Greek language shows the word angel as messenger because it assumes the word to be angels as written in English. The word has to be referenced back to its original for correct translation. Man comes from the god-class of beings. Modern day theologians and religious people reject the idea that man is in the god-class but Jesus made it clear that we are.

John 10:30-34
I and *my* Father are one. [31]Then the Jews took up stones again to stone him. [32]Jesus answered them, Many good works have I showed you from my Father; for which of those works do you stone me? [33]The Jews answered him, saying, For a good work we stone you not; but for blasphemy; and because that you, being a man, makes yourself God. [34]Jesus answered them, Is it not written in your law, I said, You are gods?

Psalm 82:1
God stands in the congregation of the mighty; he judges among the gods.

Psalm 82:6
I have said, You *are* gods; and all of you *are* children of the most High.

Most Christians would not dispute the fact that we are one with God through Jesus Christ His Son. But when Jesus said this, the religious people wanted to stone Him to death for blasphemy. They understood Him to mean that He was saying that He was God. Religious people think they same way today. They stumble over the idea and they believe that it is blasphemy to suggest that humans can be gods. One of the names of the Son of God is Emmanuel, which being interpreted means God is with us.

The Apostle Paul said that it was completely proper for us to think the same way that Jesus did.

Philippians 2:5-6

Let this mind be in you, which was also in Christ Jesus: [6]Who, being in the form of God, thought it not robbery to be equal with God:

Believers are supposed to think the same way that Jesus did. We are not equal with God in status, but we are equal with God in character, privilege and ability. Jesus thought this way as the son of man anointed by God. In other words, Jesus thought this way as a human being with the power of God upon Him. This kind of thinking is "thousandfold thinking." God does not think with limitations. God thinks with thousandfold thought. Thousandfold mindset empowers unlimited potential and ability, it is thinking in unlimited measure.

Most people have been taught that you can never know what God is thinking. Unfortunately this incorrect statement comes from incomplete teaching. A good bit of this incorrect instruction comes from a statement in the book of Isaiah.

Isaiah 55:7-9

Let the wicked forsake his way, and the unrighteous man his thoughts: and let him return unto the LORD, and he will have mercy upon him; and to our God, for he will abundantly pardon. [8]For my thoughts *are* not your thoughts, neither *are* your ways my ways, saith the LORD. [9]For *as* the heavens are higher than the earth, so are my ways higher than your ways, and my thoughts than your thoughts.

Based on verse 8 and verse 9, it would appear that you couldn't know God's thoughts or His ways. In order to fully understand the passage you must connect verse 7 to the statement. Verse 7 is speaking to the wicked and unrighteous man.

Only the unrighteous couldn't understand God's way and thoughts. A born-again Christian is the righteousness of God in Christ Jesus and has been abundantly pardoned so you can know God's thoughts and His ways. You become God's righteousness when you get saved.

After you are saved then your mind needs to be transformed to think like God does. Being transformed by the renewing of your mind is a progressive process of hearing the word of God and walking in the word.

To be transformed means to be radically changed from one state to another. The radical transformation will then open your mind to hear from the Holy Spirit and generate a whole new way of thinking.

When you were lost, your fallen mind only knew to react with fallen responses. Instead of turning the other cheek, you struck back at the person who offended you. After salvation, your mind goes through a redeveloped mental progression that sorts through the new ideas and then weighs them against the old ones. The more you hear the word of God and the more you practice what you hear, the more proficient you become in it.

Your confession of Jesus as the Son of God that rose from the dead on the third day makes you a legal citizen of the Kingdom of Heaven. The Kingdom of God is then deposited in you and old things pass away and all things become new. This pertains to your spirit. Your mind still needs quite a bit of work. The mind must be renewed just as the brain cells are replenished every day. This is where gaining the mind of Christ comes into play.

Having the mind of Christ empowers you to understand what is on the Lord's mind. The supernatural intelligence of God can flow through your mind producing a stream of the manifold wisdom of God. The manifold wisdom of God is what fills the earth full of God's riches and His mercy.

Psalm 104:24

O LORD, how manifold are Your works! in wisdom have You made them all: the earth is full of Your riches.

The word manifold is the Hebrew word Raw-bab and it means to increase by a myriad. Myriad is the word for ten thousand. King David used this word when he spoke the blessing of thousandfold increase over God's people.

Psalm 144:13

That our garners *may be* full, affording all manner of store: *that* our sheep may bring forth thousands and ten thousands in our streets:

David's prayer was for God to increase the people through a myriad of the thousandfold wisdom. God does not give you wealth, instead He gives you the wisdom to obtain it. The manifold wisdom of God will generate multiple thousandfold ideas that will pave the way to incredible wealth and riches.

The wisdom of God will give you:

- Ideas
- Insights
- Inventions
- Ingenuity

God has empowered His people to dominate financially and spiritually so that you can operate with the power of a thousandfold God! God gave you the thousandfold blessing to become fruitful and multiply for the Kingdom and to obtain the resources necessary to fulfill the preaching of the Gospel of the Kingdom of God.

This present age will close when the church has done its job. The job of the Church is to preach the Gospel to every nation so that everyone has an opportunity to receive Jesus as his or her Savior and Lord.

Mathew 24:14
And this gospel of the kingdom shall be preached in the entire world for a witness unto all nations; and then shall the end come.

The Gospel has been fully preached when the thousandfold anointing of God is released through signs, wonders and miracles. The Gospel is fully preached when all families on the earth are blessed. When people are fed, clothed, housed and loved, we have fully preached the Gospel. This is the promise that God made to His faithful friend Abraham and it is the same promise that He has made to you.

We need the thousandfold blessing of God so that we can finish the work assigned to us. From the reports of the times we live in today, it is obvious that we are in the season of Jesus return. Iniquity abounds, men call good evil and evil good.

The perilous times the Apostle Paul spoke of are upon us and we must do all that we can to bring the word of God and His glorious Kingdom into the hearts and homes of the billions of souls that are searching for life and love that comes exclusively from our Heavenly Father.

I have faith to believe that there is a remnant of people in the Church that are going to take hold of the thousandfold principle and flow with thousandfold prosperity to preach the Gospel and establish the Kingdom of God. They will be the ones that God uses for the transfer of end time wealth.

The promise of the transfer of end time wealth belongs to the Church and it is our responsibility to spoil the world of its wealth, so that the money that belongs in the Kingdom of God will flow through the hands of the children of God.

God has put forth a plan to move abundant amounts of money from the hands of the wicked to the Church for use in this present day. There are numerous promises that attest to that fact.

End time wealth transfer Scripture Verses:
- Proverbs 13:22
- James 5:1-3
- Job 20:15
- Ecclesiastes 2:26
- Isaiah 60:4-5
- Haggai 2:7-8

The key to seeing end time wealth come to the Church for the last days preaching of the Gospel is very simple. It will come to those who have qualified themselves through their giving, and have compassion for the poor and needy.

Proverbs 28:8
He that by usury and unjust gain increases his substance, he shall gather it for him that will pity the poor.

The transference of the wealth of the wicked is not an uncommon event. There are numerous examples of this taking place in the Bible:

- Abraham took all of the goods at the battle of the Kings.
- Israel left Egypt with all their wealth.
- Jacob took all the wealth of his Uncle Laban.
- David recovered all of the goods from the Amalakites.
- Jehoshaphat and Judah took all the spoils of the enemies for three days.
- Jesus spoiled the devil at the cross of Calvary.

Jesus said that the children of this world are wiser in their own ways than the children of the light. That is why you are seeing extraordinary amounts of money gathered to the large corporations and companies around the world. They use worldly wisdom to develop technology and products that generate huge profits.

It may seem that the wicked are prospering while the righteous suffer financial lack, but the word of God declares that they are doing this for Kingdom purposes.

The transfer of end time wealth does not come gradually; it will happen suddenly. Whenever the people of God spoiled their enemies they did so in a single day. God does things quickly, suddenly and immediately. When the transfer does happen there will be many rich and wealthy wicked people that will weep and howl for their miseries because they will hand it over to the people of God who will use it for God's glory.

The transfer of end time wealth will be the ultimate thousandfold increase in the Body of Christ. The way you handle money now will determine your qualification to be a part of this prophetic event. Once the money comes into the Church for the last day's harvest of souls, we will be in a position to quickly finish the assignment of the Great Commission bringing the dispensation of grace to an end.

Once the Church completes its assignment, it will be ready for the return of the Lord. God will then open the graves of the dead in Christ and rapture those who are alive to be with Him forever. Then the Great Tribulation period will begin. During that time the thousandfold principle will continue to be in force on the earth.

There will come a moment during the Great Tribulation where the Anti-Christ will sit in the Temple in Jerusalem and confess himself to be God. This will trigger a reaction from the nation of Israel and as a result of this, 144,000 Jewish people will revolt against the Anti-Christ and will begin to evangelize the world with the truth about Jesus Christ as the Messiah of the world.

Revelation 7:4-8
And I heard the number of them which were sealed: *and there were* sealed an hundred *and* forty *and* four thousand of all the tribes of the children of Israel. [5]Of the tribe of Judah *were* sealed twelve thousand. Of the tribe of Reuben *were* sealed twelve thousand. Of the tribe of Gad *were* sealed twelve

thousand. [6]Of the tribe of Aser *were* sealed twelve thousand. Of the tribe of Nepthalim *were* sealed twelve thousand. Of the tribe of Manasses *were* sealed twelve thousand. [7]Of the tribe of Simeon *were* sealed twelve thousand. Of the tribe of Levi *were* sealed twelve thousand. Of the tribe of Issachar *were* sealed twelve thousand. [8]Of the tribe of Zabulon *were* sealed twelve thousand. Of the tribe of Joseph *were* sealed twelve thousand. Of the tribe of Benjamin *were* sealed twelve thousand.

God will establish the Jewish evangelists in the Great Tribulation in ranks of thousands. This includes twelve thousand people from each of the twelve tribes of Israel. The 144,000 are used to tell the world the truth about the Anti-Christ and more importantly, the truth about Jesus Christ. This thousandfold group did not take the mark of the beast, so they are not doomed like those who will. They have been reserved for the final harvest of souls on planet earth. When Jesus returns to bring final judgment on satan, He will use the thousandfold principle to seal his doom.

Revelation 20:2-3
And he laid hold on the dragon, that old serpent, which is the devil, and satan, and bound him a thousand years, [3]And cast him into the bottomless pit, and shut him up, and set a seal upon him, that he should deceive the nations no more, till the thousand years should be fulfilled: and after that he must be loosed a little season.

God uses the thousandfold principle to terminate the devil on earth. The one thousand years serves as the divine sentence for all of the diabolical things that satan perpetrated on mankind for thousands of years. We do not know all the details of what transpired at the time satan fell but we have enough information to understand that he attempted to overthrow God from the throne and he failed. Jesus said that He saw war in Heaven and satan fell like lightning. We can gather together certain facts about satan's original form, position and purpose, and we can see a physical description of the way that God adorned him.

Ezekiel 28:12b-15

Thus says the Lord GOD; you seal up the sum, full of wisdom, and perfect in beauty. [13]you have been in Eden the garden of God; every precious stone *was* your covering, the sardius, topaz, and the diamond, the beryl, the onyx, and the jasper, the sapphire, the emerald, and the carbuncle, and gold: the workmanship of your tabrets and of your pipes was prepared in you in the day that you were created. [14]you *are* the anointed cherub that covers; and I have set you *so*: you were upon the holy mountain of God; you have walked up and down in the midst of the stones of fire. [15]you *were* perfect in your ways from the day that you were created, until iniquity was found in you.

Isaiah 14:12-15

How art you fallen from heaven, O lucifer, son of the morning! *how* art you cut down to the ground, which didst weaken the nations! [13]For you have said in your heart, I will ascend into heaven, I will exalt my throne above the stars of God: I will sit also upon the mount of the congregation, in the sides of the north: [14]I will ascend above the heights of the clouds; I will be like the most High. [15]Yet you shall be brought down to hell, to the sides of the pit.

These two passages of scripture give us a fairly decent picture of what happened when Lucifer fell. In Isaiah 14:15 satan is destined for Hell. Jesus referred to Hell as the place prepared for the devil and his angels. It is not until the book of Revelation that we see the sentence of judgment that God placed on satan.

God must have established the verdict against satan for a pre-determined time. The question that must be asked is, why didn't God eliminate satan at the time of his insurrection? After all He is God and He can do whatever He wants right? Yes, but only to the degree of His word.

We know that satan will be bound for one thousand years and then be let loose for a short period of time. Therefore, we can assume that God set an appointed time for satan to roam about the earth. There must have been some kind of compact between God and satan that gave satan the right to exist while man was given the dominion of the planet.

The logical explanation is that the time bond for satan and the introduction of man crossed over. The devil challenged man's God-given authority so that he could steal the dominion of the earth. God put man on the earth to enjoy the pleasures and privileges that God knew. God's plan for man also included three things for the destruction of satan.

A) Destroy the works of the devil
1 John 3:8
He that commits sin is of the devil; for the devil sinned from the beginning. For this purpose the Son of God was manifested, that he might destroy the works of the devil.

B) Remove the power of death from the devil
Hebrews 2:14b-15
...that through death he might destroy him that had the power of death, that is, the devil; [15]And deliver them who through fear of death were all their lifetime subject to bondage.

C) Spoil the devil of all his goods
Colossians 2:15
And having spoiled principalities and powers, he made a show of them openly, triumphing over them in it.

Adam did not fulfill the original assignment in the Garden of Eden when he was told to guard and defend the planet. God gave Adam authority over everything that moved upon the earth. The devil came into the garden through the body of the serpent when he came to beguile Adam. Adam could have been used as the bounty hunter who would have brought satan to an end if he had not listened to the words of the serpent and sinned. That is why God sent Jesus to finish the job as the last Adam.

1 Corinthians 15:45-47
And so it is written, the first man Adam was made a living soul; the last Adam *was made* a quickening spirit. [46]Howbeit that *was* not first which is spiritual, but that which is natural; and afterward that which is spiritual. [47]The first man *is* of the earth, earthy: the second man *is* the Lord from heaven.

Thank God for the plan of salvation and redemption that the precious blood of Jesus provides for the whole human race! We have been given a decisive victory over sin, death, the grave and Hell itself because of the triumph of the Cross of Calvary.

During the one thousand years that satan is bound, the Church will reign and rule with the Lord for one thousand years. The one thousand year reign is the product of the thousandfold principle. It will be exactly one thousand years that God places the resurrected Church on the earth with Jesus.

Revelation 20:4-6

Then I saw thrones, and sitting on them were those who had been given the right to judge. And I saw the souls of those who had been beheaded for their testimony about Jesus, for proclaiming the Word of God, and who had not worshiped the Creature or his statue, nor accepted his mark on their foreheads or their hands. They had come to life again and now they reigned with Christ for a thousand years. [5]This is the First Resurrection. (The rest of the dead did not come back to life until the thousand years had ended.) [6]Blessed and holy are those who share in the First Resurrection. For them the Second Death holds no terrors, for they will be priests of God and of Christ, and shall reign with him a thousand years.

What will the Church do with Jesus during the one thousand years? We will learn how to operate as kings and priests do. We will learn how to live and function in complete and total peace. We will enter into the rest of God and become everything that we were originally designed to be but without fear, sorrow, sin, or death.

There will continue to be people on the earth during the one thousand years, known as the Millennial Peace. Time continues on the earth for one thousand years.

This Millennial generation will grow up as the thousandfold generation. The thousandfold principle will produce a generation of people on the earth without hatred, murder, abortion, or any other diabolical work of the flesh. The thousandfold principle produces a people with unlimited life and freedom. The center of the thousandfold generation is

Jesus. He is the source of light and life that unifies the people into one nation under God.

When the thousand years has ended, satan is loosed for a little season. No one knows how long this will be but we do know what he is doing during this time. He is organizing the armies of Gog and Magog to fight against Jesus and the Saints known as the Elect.

Revelation 20:7-10
And when the thousand years are expired, satan shall be loosed out of his prison, [8]And shall go out to deceive the nations which are in the four quarters of the earth, Gog and Magog, to gather them together to battle: the number of whom *is* as the sand of the sea. [9]And they went up on the breadth of the earth, and compassed the camp of the saints about, and the beloved city: and fire came down from God out of heaven, and devoured them. [10]And the devil that deceived them was cast into the lake of fire and brimstone, where the beast and the false prophet *are*, and shall be tormented day and night for ever and ever.

The devil meets his final demise and is thrown into the lake of fire with the beast and the false prophet. The thousandfold Kingdom of God has overthrown satan's kingdom with the thousandfold anointing of a thousand generation. The fact that these prophecies are written down is proof that we win and satan loses.

The thousandfold principle is an unstoppable, unlimited force of power that transcends time and releases the unlimited measure of God's ability to overcome every enemy and any obstacle in your way.

Chapter 12

Thousandfold Love

John 3:16

For God so loved the world that He gave His only begotten Son, that whoever believes in Him should not perish but have everlasting life.

The love of God is what saved the world. God's love is unlimited love for mankind traveled through a microscopic seed to grow for nine months in the womb of a young woman named Mary. God chose to send His only begotten Son into the world so that you could call upon the name of Jesus and be saved.

God's thousandfold desire was the driving force that brought the plan of salvation to pass. The saving power of God operates in the thousandfold measure. After Jesus resurrected from the dead, He ascended to the Throne of God in Heaven. Fifty days afterwards on the Day of Pentecost the Holy Spirit was sent and poured out upon all flesh.

The Holy Spirit came into the Upper Room and baptized the 120 men and women. Then they all spoke in tongues and prophesied as tongues of fire appeared above their heads. The sound of the rushing mighty wind of the Holy Spirit caused the nations to run to see what was causing the noise.

The Apostle Peter preached to the gathering crowd and as a result of his invitation people came to the Lord by the thousands.

Acts 2:41 NKJV

Then they that gladly received his word were baptized: and the same day there were added *unto them* about **three thousand souls**.

Acts 4:4 NKJV

However, many of those who heard the word believed; and the number of the men came to be about **five thousand**.

The thousandfold love of God is the force behind the salvation of souls by the thousands. This is the way that God will harvest souls in the last day, by thousandfold measure. The Church has the technological tools at its disposal to complete the task of preaching the Gospel to the nations.

There are over 35 Christian TV networks around the world proclaiming the word of the Lord to billions of souls around the clock. The Internet has accelerated the ability to communicate like never before and soon wireless will open new opportunities we have yet to embark upon.

The thing that is lacking is the momentum of the thousandfold principle operating in the Body of Christ. When the Church takes hold of the thousandfold principle then we will have more than adequate supply of love, power and wisdom to complete the assignment of preaching the Gospel of the Kingdom to all of the people in all of the nations.

The single most important message of the Gospel is the fact that God loves you and that He sent His Son Jesus to save you from eternal damnation. The revelation of the love of God for you is what will transform your life and radically change the way you live and think forever.

I have covered the various facets of the subject of the thousandfold principle including wisdom, faith and prosperity. All of them are a product of the covenant of God's word that is given to a thousand generations.

Deuteronomy 7:9
Know therefore that the LORD your God, he *is* God, the faithful God, which keeps covenant and mercy with them that love him and keep his commandments to a thousand generations;

The covenant agreement of mercy and forgiveness is based on your love for God and willingness to keep His commandments. A command is designated to place and keep order in life. Before the curse of sin came into the world there was only one commandment that God originally gave to mankind. That single commandment was not difficult to keep as long as Adam trusted God and listened to His voice.

Genesis 2:15-17
And the LORD God took the man, and put him into the Garden of Eden to dress it and to keep it. [16]And the LORD God commanded the man, saying, Of every tree of the garden you may freely eat: [17]But of the tree of the knowledge of good and evil, you shall not eat of it: for in the day that you eat thereof you shall surely die.

The word commanded means to constitute, appoint and join together. Constitute is the root word for constitution. A constitution is the declared or written law of the land. Whatever the constitution says becomes the protocol for the way things are done legally and lawfully. The constitution sets the standard for a nation.

The Constitution of the United States is one of the strongest man-made documents in history. The citizens of the U.S.A. are all expected to live by the Constitution as one nation under God. The citizens that keep the commandments of the country get to enjoy the benefits of the pursuit of life and liberty. Those citizens that do not keep the commands are subject to the penalties of breaking the law.

God's first commandment was for man to simply enjoy the good things that God put on the earth for them to partake of. He said to freely eat from all of the trees He planted except for the tree of the knowledge of good and evil. You would think that being commanded to eat would come easy, but eating the right thing is not always so simple.

One command with many benefits

All Adam had to do was to guard and defend the Garden of Eden from any and all predators including satan. Adam was assigned the task of "Garden Security." His job description required him to use his God-given authority to drive out and overcome anything that moved in opposition to his power. The devil was looking for a way to steal the privileges given to Adam, and he came through a serpent to entice Adam female to look at and think about eating the fruit of the tree of the knowledge of good and evil.

The woman ate the fruit and then gave it to the man, and he did eat. Both of them fell under the curse of sin and death. Adam's disobedience to listen and trust God's word resulted in a death sentence for the whole human race. God quickly entered into the matter and made a seed faith promise to bring Jesus through the woman. He is the seed that crushed the serpent's head, which took back the authority that man had in the beginning.

Before salvation in the name of Jesus, God gave mankind the law or Torah. This was introduced because of sin. Moses gave the law to Israel so they would not transgress the commandments of God. There were a total of 613 laws that dealt with matters pertaining to spiritual, civil, dietary, and sanitation issues. 613 commandments is a lot to remember every day no matter how good your memory or will power is.

The Bible states that if you broke one of the laws, then you broke all of the laws. In order to simplify things for God's people, Moses brought forth the Ten Commandments written by the finger of God on tablets of stone. These ten commands categorized all of the 613 laws.

Keeping the Ten Commandments would essentially fulfill all of the hundreds of laws because the ten are the foundation for the 613. Remember, mankind started with just one commandment and then graduated to 613. God condensed the 613 laws into the Ten Commandments. You have to admit that keeping the 10 commands would be easier than keeping the 613 commands.

The sacrificial blood system was introduced in the Garden of Eden to cover the sins of the people because people struggle and fall short of the glory of God. The blood of innocent animals would eternally be used to satisfy the penalty of sin. Under the Law of Moses the blood of bulls, goats and sheep only covered the sins of the people.

God sent Jesus as the Lamb of God that was sent to take away the sins of the world. The difference is between covering and taking away. To cover something suggests that the sin remained but was shielded by the blood. This system of sacrifice in the Old Testament made it necessary to continually offer blood to God for the sins committed by the people throughout the year.

The blood of Jesus did not cover the sin, it took it away once and for all. The blood of Jesus blotted out the sin and the power of death that it once had. Jesus took away the fear and power of death from satan at the Cross of Calvary.

Jesus sacrificial offering was sufficient to remove the sins of the entire human race that came through Adam. Through Adam all died because of sin but through Jesus all live because He gave His life to pay for the sin, or debt, we owed. God accepted His offering in Heaven and on Earth eternally. That makes the blood of Jesus a thousandfold offering because there is no limit on the number of souls that can come through the plan of salvation!

Through the grace and mercy of the Lord Jesus Christ the law that was once against us was fulfilled and the handwriting of the law was removed.

Colossians 2:13-15

And you, being dead in your sins and the uncircumcision of your flesh, has he quickened together with him, having forgiven you all trespasses; [14]Blotting out the handwriting of ordinances that was against us, which was contrary to us, and took it out of the way, nailing it to his cross; [15]And having spoiled principalities and powers, he made a show of them openly, triumphing over them in it.

The body of Jesus was removed from the cross but the nails remained embedded in it. The nails will forever hold the law that was against you on the backside of the cross. The cross performs the function as the instrument of unlimited thousandfold forgiveness, grace and mercy. The nails of the cross were not an afterthought in the mind of God. The nails were forethought in the plan of redemption.

In the Garden of Eden there were three things mentioned in the land of Havilah that play an important role in man's future. They include: gold, bdellium and the onyx stone.

Genesis 2:11-12
The name of the first *is* Pison: that *is* it which compassed the whole land of Havilah, where *there is* gold; [12]And the gold of that land *is* good: there *is* bdellium and the onyx stone.

The onyx stone in the Hebrew translation means a nail. God symbolically placed the nails in the Garden as a safeguard for the salvation of mankind. According to the Smith's Bible Dictionary, the onyx is not a transparent stone, but as the color of the flesh appears through the nail (Greek onyx) on the human body, so the reddish mass which is below shines delicately through the whitish surface of the onyx. In other words, the stone has the reflection of flesh tone with blood running in it. This portrays the piercing of Jesus body for your sins.

Interestingly the onyx stone is found on the garments of the High Priest. There are exactly three stones on the robe that they wore before the Lord when serving in the Tabernacle or Sanctuary. This parallels the three nails that Jesus took in his hands and in his feet. Two of the three onyx stones on the High

Priest garments were located on both of the shoulders and the third stone was located on the bottom center of the breastplate. Notice that the onyx stones were laid out in the general location that the nails were when they pierced His hands and feet. The nails are evidence of the removal of the power of sin against you, and the holes in the hands of Jesus are a reminder of the New Covenant you have with God.

After Jesus came back from the dead, He appeared to His disciples on three different occasions. On one occasion He appears to the disciples in a room they were hiding in from the Jews. Thomas, or Didymus which means twin, was there with them. Thomas was known as a doubter because he required physical evidence to believe in something. Even his name speaks of the double nature of his mind and heart. Jesus knew that Thomas had said that he would not believe Jesus was alive unless he could put his finger in the nail prints of Jesus hands.

Jesus told Thomas to place his finger in His hands. In essence Jesus showed Thomas His wounds and Thomas then believed that it was the Lord. Jesus said that those who have not seen and yet believe are blessed. It is to be noted that the prints in the hands of Jesus came from the nails on the cross. It is equally interesting to note that the finger has a nail of its own. We call it a fingernail. The fingernail of Thomas would point to the location where the wound was. Thomas wanted to touch the wounds with his own hands.

The pointed finger is the figure of judgment. Thomas wanted to judge the body of Jesus by thrusting his fingernail in the hole of the wound. The good news is that you are a part of the Body of Christ. You are no longer subject to the judgment of people nor are you subject to the judgment of sin or the death it produces. The fingernail of judgment will always point to the nail prints in the hands of Jesus.

Jesus took the sins of the whole world and the iniquity of us all was laid upon Him. When Jesus completed the work of Calvary, He fulfilled the law that was against you. The unmerited, unlimited, thousandfold grace of God was offered to you so that you would no longer owe anything to the sin. From the point that you accept the salvation of the Lord, you only owe one thing because the blood of Jesus Christ has paid the debt.

Romans 13:8-10

Owe no man any thing, but to love one another: for they that love another have fulfilled the law. ^{9}For this, You shall not commit adultery, You shall not kill, You shall not steal, You shall not bear false witness, You shall not covet; and if *there be* any other commandment, it is briefly comprehended in this saying, namely, You shall love your neighbor as yourself. ^{10}Love works no ill to their neighbor: therefore love *is* the fulfilling of the law.

Before Jesus went to the Cross, He gave the New Commandment for the Church, the Body of Christ.

John13:34-35

A new commandment I give unto you, that you love one another; as I have loved you, that you also love one another. ^{35}By this shall all *people* know that you are my disciples, if you have love one to another.

This new commandment was given by Jesus as the one commandment that you must keep in order to stay in covenant with God. Keeping this new commandment will fulfill the entire

Law of God. When you walk in the love of God it causes you to fulfill the Ten Commandments because you no longer want to break the law.

The Ten Commandments were compacted into one new commandment. This made it much easier to keep the commandments. So mankind started with one commandment and finished with one commandment. It breaks down like this:

- 1 Commandment in the Garden of Eden.
  - o Freely enjoy all of the trees of the Garden but don't eat from the Tree of the Knowledge of Good and Evil.
- 613 Laws, statutes and ordinances in the Law of Moses.
  - o Hundreds of spiritual, civil, dietary, and sanitary laws.
- 10 Commandments covering the 613 Laws of Moses.
  - o Written in stone by the finger of God.
- 1 New Commandment to walk in love like Jesus did.
  - o Written on the heart of the Believer.

You may have a number of things in your life that you need to work on, but if you work on walking in love then all of the other things will come into line for you. God simplified the process of keeping His commandments by providing His love for you through Jesus.

In the Garden of Eden mankind only had to keep the commandment of enjoying the good things that God gave them to enjoy. Walking in love returns you back to the original commandment of unlimited thousandfold blessing and increase.

Many people struggle with communicating love to others. The key to giving and receiving love with others is to accept the love of God for you. Accepting the thousandfold love of God is

226

the beginning of the transformation of your life. Having a revelation of the love of God will change your heart and make your life whole. In order to change you must fall in love with the Lord Jesus.

Loving the Lord is the most important thing that you will ever do in your entire life. Loving God is an essential key to flowing in the thousandfold principle. King Solomon's thousandfold dream seed was founded upon his love for God and God's love for him.

1 Kings 3:3-4
And **Solomon loved the LORD**, walking in the statutes of David his father: only he sacrificed and burnt incense in high places. [4]And the king went to Gibeon to sacrifice there; for that *was* the great high place: a thousand burnt offerings did Solomon offer upon that altar.

2 Samuel 12:24
And David comforted Bathsheba his wife, and went in unto her, and lay with her: and she bore a son, and he called his name Solomon: and **the LORD loved him**.

The love between Solomon and God was the binding agent of the thousandfold dream and the thousandfold wisdom and prosperity that the Lord gave to Solomon. The love between you and God will be the same thing. Without love there is no foundation to stand upon. God loves you with an everlasting and unlimited love that can withstand the trials and tests that this world has to offer.

Thousandfold Lifestyle

John 10:10

The thief does not come except to steal, and to kill, and to destroy. I have come that they may have life, and that they may have *it* more abundantly.

Amplified

The thief comes only in order to steal and kill and destroy. I came that they may have *and* enjoy life, and have it in abundance (to the full, till it overflows).

Jesus said that He came to give you abundant life. The Amplified Bible says that He came to give you life overflowing. Jesus did not die and return from the grave just to give you a life insurance policy. Thank God the plan of salvation promises eternal life with Him. Your experience of eternal life does not have to wait until you die and go to Heaven, you can begin living the life right now!

Eternal life is a quality of life that lasts for eternity. Many of the Christians that I have ministered to know they were going to Heaven when they died but they were living their life like Hell on Earth. God does not want you to go to Hell, nor does He want you to go through it to get to Heaven.

When Israel left Egypt, God made a promise to bring them into land flowing with good and plentiful things. He promised to remove sickness and disease from their midst and to make the days that they lived on Earth as if they were the days of Heaven on Earth. A real relationship with Jesus will open the door for an unlimited thousandfold lifestyle that will take off the limits of this world and release the power and anointing of the thousandfold Kingdom of God forever in your life.

When you give your life to the Lord you become a child of God and a part of His glorious Kingdom. The Holy Spirit will pour His thousandfold presence into your life on a daily basis, which will cause a flood of God's love, light and liberty to flow through your spirit. You have to make the first step towards God and come to Him unashamedly just as you are. I encourage you to make more than a decision to become a Christian,

I encourage you to become a full-fledged Believer that accepts the forgiveness for all of your sins from the past, present and future. I encourage you to invite the Holy Spirit to fill your heart every day with the thousandfold love of the Father in Heaven so that you will not have to be ashamed again. I encourage you to ask the Holy Spirit to baptize you with His Spirit and with fire to build you and strengthen you with boldness, courage and ability.

If you have never given your heart to the Lord, or if you have given your heart to Him but have not lived the good, eternal and thousandfold lifestyle He has promised you, please take some quality time and go to God and ask for Him to enter into your life today. God has already forgiven you of all of your sins; now all you must do is accept this fact and then confess your sins to God. He is faithful to cleanse you of all of your sins and to give you a brand new start.

Ask Jesus to come into your heart and He will make you a brand new person. God will then begin the process of transforming you into a thousandfold believer that will propel you into the greatest lifestyle you could ever live, the thousandfold lifestyle.

Pray this prayer out loud:

Heavenly Father, I come to You today to ask You for forgiveness of all my sins and I accept Your forgiveness and the love that You have for me. Please come into my life and make me a brand new person today. I believe Jesus is the Son of God, God raised Him from the dead on the third day and I confess this now as a Born-Again child of God. Holy Spirit I invite You to fill my heart with the love of the Father and to baptize me with Your Spirit and Your fire. I make a commitment to serve you with all my heart, I ask You to lead me and guide me in all truth and to teach me how to live for You Lord. I thank You for the gift of salvation and for all the gifts that You bestow upon me. In Jesus Name, amen.

If you prayed this prayer, please let me know so I can rejoice with you and keep you in prayer.

Website: www.johnwsmithjr.com

Phone: U.S. toll free 877-597-9595

Outside U.S.   812-949-9595

Address: P.O. Box 2605 Clarksville, Indiana 47131 U.S.A.

Final Thoughts

The thousandfold principle is capable of accomplishing the impossible and revealing the invisible. I hope by now your faith and imagination have been stretched beyond their limits and are now reaching the astounding revelation of the amazing, super-intelligent God of all creation. I learned all of these lessons by revelation of the Holy Spirit and with a thousandfold seed sown into the Kingdom of God. I challenge you to take hold of the thousandfold principle and I further dare you to act on the principle right now.

I encourage you to consider sowing a thousandfold seed today. I firmly believe that the impartation of instruction will take effect when you sow a seed with the person who teaches you. If this book has enlightened your understanding, consider sowing a thousandfold seed with my ministry.

Many of the people that I have taught this lesson to through the years have sown the thousandfold seed and have seen God perform amazing miracles for them. When you give be sure and state what the thousandfold seed represents so that I can agree with you in prayer.

You can sow your thousandfold seed several different ways:

Website: www.johnwsmithjr.com

U.S. toll free   877-597-9595

Outside U.S.   812-949-9595

Address: P.O. Box 2605 Clarksville, Indiana 47131 U.S.A.

God bless you for taking the time to read this book. I look forward to hearing from you soon. I pray that God bless the work of your hands a THOUSANDFOLD!

Pastor John W. Smith, Jr.